woke

Change your perception
Change your self
Change your life

MICHAEL DYER

Copyright © 2019 Michael Dyer

ISBN: 9781099148231

Book designed and edited by Joanna Pounds Simpson
Cover design by Todd Westover

www.coachwithzen.com
mdyerwoke@gmail.com

This book is dedicated to my grandmother Estelle Tate who took me into her home and heart and loved me unconditionally. It is dedicated to all the souls who challenged me to seek within, my Spiritual guides who have guided my steps and opened doors of opportunity so that I might walk through them. This is dedicated to you, the seeker, for without you this book could not exist.

Table of Contents

woke

urban dictionary definitions:

woke
/wōk/
verb

1. past of wake.

   adjective
   informal • US
   adjective: **woke**; comparative adjective: **woker**;
   superlative adjective: **wokest**

2. Spiritual and intellectual enlightenment, like
   waking up from a deep sleep and seeing things
   clearly for the first time.
   I never knew what really mattered in life. Now I'm woke.

3. A word used to describe "consciousness" and
   being aware of the truth behind things.

introduction

It seems like just yesterday that I was attending a life mastery class and gathered up the courage to stand up with a microphone to speak my truth in front of two hundred classmates. My words were unscripted—I just spoke from my heart—and, afterward, many of my classmates came up and hugged me. They thanked me for sharing my experiences, and I felt so loved and appreciated! I also felt embarrassed and ashamed because what they saw in me, I didn't see. They saw me as this powerful, loving, sensitive, and strong soul. Some of them wanted to spend time with me and help me realize my dreams because they believed in me even though I didn't believe in myself.

I began to cry because there was a room full of people who saw something great in me that I didn't even see in myself. So I wondered, "Why aren't I able to see my own light? Why can't I see my own beauty? Why don't I love myself?" I had shared my shortcomings and things I was ashamed of and didn't want anybody to know and, yet, they loved and accepted me. At that moment, I realized I was very critical of myself, that I was my greatest enemy. I asked myself over and over again why I couldn't see my own light or feel my own power. How could I be blind to my very essence?

As I was observing my friends' dogs and cats, the answer flooded in. The animals didn't recognize their reflections. Some of them even went into attack mode when seeing them. I realized that they didn't see themselves the way I see myself. They didn't see themselves at all—they were just in a state of being themselves—and I realized we are not here to judge ourselves, but to be ourselves.

We are like the sun. It cannot see its radiant light nor feel its mighty heat, and yet it is the source of life on earth. No one can deny the power of the sun. Like the sun, we were meant to let our light shine for the world to behold and for our presence to be felt, to let the clouds of doubt and fear disappear so that we may witness the effects of our magnificent power. Imagine a world without a mirror. We wouldn't know what we looked like and therefore, all judgment about appearance would disappear.

At that moment, I thought, "Without the judgment of people, who would I be? Who could I be?" I would be just like the sun emanating my light throughout the universe. At that moment, this book was born; I was reborn without any limitations. I, the man with dyslexia, would be a writer. I would be a speaker and share my message of hope and motivation with the world!

There exists a power of influence outside of your everyday awareness but not outside of your *Authentic Self* that is the source of your breath and heartbeat. It is the invisible force that moves and exists in everything, the essence of your being-ness and where the highest part of you exists. You are being awakened right now by this invisible force that is all around you.

You are being called to trust in a power greater than the seeming power of the physical world. You are being guided from within to be mindful, to focus and seek this inner source of energy that dwells deep within and all around you. It is saying, "You are more than this seeming problem or challenge. You are more than your history. You are more than any abuse committed to your mental, emotional, or physical body. You are more than this thing called life. You are more than your education or lack thereof. You are more than the crimes and mistakes you have committed. You are more than the crimes and mistakes that were committed against you. You are more than the disappointment and shame in your past."

Who you are cannot be labeled or defined by others. The world's labels do not possess meaning in the inner world where pure divine energy resides. Who you are in truth and where you came from cannot be fully explained or proven by the world. Your true identity dwells in a place beyond description. And yet, you have come to a world where labels are used to organize, create structure, and give meaning to your life. If we did not place labels on people, places, and things, life would have no context. Name brands, physical attributes, and polarizing classifications such as *dumb, smart, poor, rich, good,* and *bad* would be meaningless. Everything you have an emotional attachment to would lose its power of influence, and you would not be affected by what people think of you. Memories would be rendered irrelevant. Imagine the freedom!

As you wake up to the truth of your authentic self, you will discover that you have unconsciously ascribed to the world all of the meaning it has for you. You have done this based upon conditioning and environmental programming as well as the painfully crafted stories of worthlessness or self-value you have been telling yourself. You have chosen to exist in a world where, for the most part, having approval, status, and money are deemed ultra-important, and for many people, have become the primary reason for existing. You may have bought into the values and norms taught to you by your family and by society at large. You have been socialized into believing what is right or wrong, and good or bad. But, throughout time, these ideas and beliefs about values and acceptable behaviors have been changing, and they are dependent on the culture within which they exist. What is acceptable in one culture may be unacceptable in another.

For example, it was considered inappropriate for women to wear pants at the turn of the century, whereas today, pants are an acceptable form of attire for women in most societies. (Although some still deem it necessary for women to cover their bodies completely). It has been the norm for human beings to own other humans, or to eat particular living organisms. Who enslaves whom and which creatures are to be ingested has fluctuated over time.

While many people in a particular society adopt a certain accepted belief pattern, there are always those who question what they are taught and form their own conclusions. They deconstruct their "old" beliefs and create new ones that are more in alignment. An important factor in this is that, as people, we have given the world all the meaning that it has for us. I was a student of *A Course In Miracles,* and one of the first "lessons" is noticing that a chair is not a chair, it is an object that we have ascribed attributes and defined as a chair. We see everything through our perceptual filters. We have created our world within our consciousness and projected it onto the outside world. Now it is time to dismantle these constructs one-by-one, thought-by-thought. *Woke* is a blueprint for doing precisely that.

Who am I to devise such a plan? How is it that I have come to know what I know and be who I am? According to the world, there is no earthly reason why you should even be reading these words! Learning to read and write was a Herculean task for me as a child since I had dyslexia. I struggled through school and, even today, I sometimes shudder at the thought of reading aloud. But I had a strong will to survive despite and because of the fear. I believe we attract miracles in our lives because I am a miracle. I have no conscious idea how the string of events that is my life manifested, making my reality what it is today.

I believe in faith, knowing that something will manifest without having to know how. I do not have everything that I want (or think I want), but I am grateful for all that I have and how it came to be. I'm profoundly thankful for the so-called "chance" meetings that have directed my life from one point to the next, the people, places and things I could never have brought together of my own volition. All I had to do was believe, surrender, trust my inner guidance, and tap into pure divine energy. It will guide our lives when we allow it, and it is what is writing this book.

My life is an example of this divine power. I came from infinite source. I am it, and it is who I am even though I grew up believing the lie that I had nothing and therefore was nothing. I discovered that you do not need to know all the steps to achieve your definition of success, you just need to believe in yourself, put one foot in front of the other, and get on to stepping. The path will be revealed to you by the same invisible force that created the universe.

In the following pages are stories about my life and my path, which I hope will inspire and uplift you. There will be examples of other divine humans who have transformed their lives and overcome seemingly insurmountable obstacles. Blessings on your journey!

1

wake up

"It is better to believe than to disbelieve; in doing you bring everything to the realm of possibility." -Albert Einstein

It's time to ask yourself, "What do I love to do more than anything? Who do I dream of being and are there roadblocks standing in my way?" No matter what obstacles appear to be blocking your path, no one can keep you from living your dream but YOU. You can be, do, and have anything that you can imagine. But first, you have to be willing to choose high vibrational thoughts. You must be willing to release any limiting beliefs about yourself and the world around you that push you into mediocrity rather than pull you towards excellence. You have to be brave enough to excel because it's much easier to be mediocre than it is to soar. Your choice to read this book indicates that you are ready to reach for the stars and realize your full potential, to achieve greatness.

Woke can help you create a life filled with possibilities

and opportunities. It will show how to tap into source energy to become the absolute best you can be. As part of this journey, you are being asked to remember you are the master of your fate and to take full responsibility for it. The more you become aware of these insights and practice embodying these principles, the more likely you'll be to experience happiness, love, peace, joy, and abundance in your life. You'll recognize that your real identity is pure divine energy with unlimited potential.

The *real* truth is that brilliance, beauty, and power are at the core of your being, no matter what has happened or is happening in the external world. Old thought patterns and stories you have been telling yourself about limitation will be sacrificed so you can put all your energy and focus into attaining your dreams. You will explore your purpose and gifts.

We are not victims. Everything we have is a result of our decisions. We are powerful creators. For me, Muhammad Ali has always been a role model because he knew that he wasn't a victim, that there was something inside of him that was great and powerful. Not even a nation could bully him into fighting for something he didn't believe in. He was willing to go to jail and forfeit his career rather than fight in what he thought to be an unjust war. His actions were in alignment with his beliefs.

This journey will be primarily about opening up your eyes to the gifts and talents that you already have. It will be about releasing old stories and negative belief patterns. It will be about tapping into Spirit and realizing that your gifts belong to the world. When we think of achieving our goals as serving the world, it helps us tap into a higher power. When we make the world the recipient of our gifts, it takes our egos out of the equation and puts tons of energy and motivation at our disposal.

affirmations

Take a moment to put your hand on your heart and get in touch with your higher self. Say these affirmations aloud:

I am pure divine energy, creating possibilities and opportunities with the willingness to win.

I take full responsibility for my life and my unlimited potential.

I am expressing all my gifts and talents, recognizing that it is my role to give and the earth's role to rejoice in my gifts. It is my role to share and the earth's role to receive.

I accept from the earth prosperity, love, and faith, knowing these gifts are a reflection of what is in my heart!

I am an amazing creator. I will let my light shine like the sun!

Our thoughts create our present lives and our futures. Your life is a direct reflection of your beliefs—no exceptions. As the Bible says, "It's done unto you as you believe." If you want to know what you have believed about your life and what you believed you deserve, all you have to do is look at your current situation and how you feel about it.

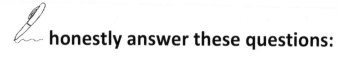

honestly answer these questions:

Are you manifesting abundance?

Are you attracting love and friendship?

Are you doing work you love?

Do you feel love and respect for yourself?

Do you feel love and respect for those around you?

Do you have inner peace?

Are you happy with the way your life has turned out?

Do you believe you can transform your life?

Are you ready for a HUGE transformation?

What are some of the areas you would like to transform?

You are living the story you have been telling yourself without knowing that you can tell a different story. You can change your future now by changing what you are saying to yourself and believing about yourself. Rewrite your story. You are the scriptwriter and the leading character! Write the character description and set the stage. Choose how you want to respond and react to the characters and situations in your life. You get to decide how much integrity you have!

> "Every choice you have ever made has led you to this moment. You have chosen every feeling and therefore created every situation in your life even if you believe you have not. You have chosen what you think, do and feel. These choices reflect the dominant ideas in your mind and therefore, create each moment. Who you believe yourself to be will influence the decisions you make in life."
> - *A Course in Miracles*

your mind is your tool

You can use your mind as a powerful tool for your advancement. A trained mind with a great imagination has unlimited potential. The more you know about a subject, the more the world opens up for you.

The Latin word for "educate," *ducere,* means "to draw out from within." A great teacher can uncover the master within the student, and a student can call forth the master within himself by tapping into the power of the imagination.

Woke is the doorway to your unlimited potential, and your vision is the master key. No one can open this door for you or stand in your way. It doesn't matter how big or powerful the obstacles may appear, they have no power over you.

You can play small and act like you don't have the master key if you choose, but know that it is merely a game you've decided to play. You can believe in a version of yourself that is scared, shy, weak, unpopular or who gets bullied and keep telling yourself the story about all the bad things that happened to you and that you can't stand up for yourself, or you can release the need for outside validation. Decide that you approve of yourself, and in doing so, be an inspiration for others to believe in themselves as well. By being the light, you will be bringing the light for others. Your empowerment will empower them!

> "Reach high, for stars lie hidden
> in your soul. Dream deep, for every
> dream precedes the goal."
> *-Pamela Vaull Starr*

be the leader & the player

You have a valuable leading role in this movie called "Your Life," and without you, it is incomplete. Everything you do or don't do has a chain reaction that ripples throughout the universe. There is a divine orchestration that is set in motion on your behalf right now based on your self-concept and choices. Situations and circumstances are occurring, and conscious and unconscious decisions are being made now because you were born. All these things are being considered and lined up perfectly for your highest good. Everything and everyone in the universe has come together in order for one single event to occur in your life.

We are more than our physical bodies; our bodies are just the houses of our souls. William Wordsworth put it beautifully when he wrote the lines:

"Our birth is but a sleep and a forgetting;
The Soul that rises with us, our life's Star,
Hath had elsewhere its setting
And cometh from afar;
Not in entire forgetfulness,
And not in utter nakedness,
But trailing clouds of glory do we come
From God, who is our home"

If we consider that the body is the home of the soul, it frees us up to reflect that our life may be just a dream. Perhaps we don't have to take it so seriously. Can you give yourself a break? If you consider that your soul has come into this existence as it may have many times before in many lives, to have an experience as a human, it offers a new paradigm in which to look at life. The experiences we are having in this human form don't have to define us. If we are souls and our experiences are happening on the human level, then it gives us a "get out of jail free" card. What happens on the human level has to get resolved on the human level, but we don't have to assign it more meaning than it deserves. We don't have to judge ourselves harshly or even judge ourselves at all. We are humans. We will make what the world calls "errors"—it's a byproduct of being human—but our souls remain intact no matter what we do. Our souls remains love and light, no matter what our human forms get up to!

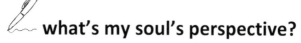

what's my soul's perspective?

If you were to consider that your soul chose to come into a human form, specifically into YOUR body, what might it be here to learn or do?

change your perspective

Can you look at your actions from a higher perspective? Can you see yourself the way God sees you? Can you see your self the way your dog sees you? An essential step to changing your life is getting out of your prejudiced thinking—the thinking you have that is against YOU. If you raise your perspective and look at an issue you are having from a different level, it can look dramatically different.

On a piece of paper, write out your "story." Now, rewrite

it! Change the story so it supports you! What is great about you? How can you redefine everything that has happened to you as supportive experiences that have made you a richer, better-equipped person for helping others?

My old story:

My rewrite:

consider these quotes:

"We are unlimited beings. We have no ceiling. The capabilities and the talents and the gifts and the power that is within every single individual that is on this planet is unlimited."
- Dr. Reverend Michael Beckwith

"The beauty you see inside me is a reflection of you." - Rumi

"Whatever your discipline, become a student of excellence in all things. Take every opportunity to observe people who manifest the qualities of mastery. These models of excellence will inspire and guide you toward the fulfillment of your highest potential."
- Tony Buzan

"You're broadcasting a signal in every moment of your existence. Your present and future circumstances begin to change in response to the signal you are offering now. And so, the entire universe, right now, is affected by what you are offering." - Abraham Hicks

"No matter what the level of your ability, you have more potential than you can ever develop in a lifetime."
- James T McCay

"You have to think big to be big." - Claude M. Bristol

"Ever since I was a child I have had this instinctive urge for expansion and growth. To me, the function and duty of a quality human being is the sincere and honest development of one's potential." - Bruce Lee

"Deep within man dwell those slumbering powers; powers that would astonish him, that he never dreamed of possessing; forces that would revolutionize his life if aroused and put into action."
- Orison Swett Marden

2

the beginning

"First comes thought; then organization of that thought, into ideas and plans; then transformation of those plans into reality. The beginning, as you will observe, is in your imagination."
- Napoleon Hill

Is it possible to be abandoned by your mother and father and still believe you are worthy of love? Is it possible to believe in yourself when no one else believes in you? Is it possible to thrive when you believe that you have nothing to live for? Is it possible to let go of victimhood after being victimized as a child? Is it possible to rise from the depths of poverty and claim victory after being homeless? Is it possible to overcome depression and suicidal thoughts? Is it possible to be labeled as worthless, lazy, and mentally challenged and still reach for and achieve success?

I am living proof that it is, and if it is true for me, it can be for you, too! The choice is yours. Will you become the living proof that it is possible? Will you allow your inherent truths to reveal themselves through the twists and turns of your life? Will you make it possible even if others may say it is impossible for you?

As a child, it seemed like I had no possibility. I couldn't perceive any future at all. I was abandoned by my parents when I was a newborn and raised by my maternal grandmother. Many of my basic needs of clothing and food were barely met. When I was three years old, I was stabbed in the head by one of my cousins who were playing with knives, an incident that had long-term ramifications. Because of my head wound, I stuttered and had difficulty remembering things and focusing so I was labeled "developmentally delayed."

My report cards seemed to confirm this diagnosis; they were terrible. I watched my classmates advance to the next grades as I was left behind. I wasn't smart enough to keep up with the others. I felt so ashamed to be labeled as the slowest kid in the class that I would either pretend to be sick or hide behind an old refrigerator on the side of the house so I wouldn't have to go to school. Shaking and crying, I prayed that no one would find me and make me go back to that horrible place. Understandably, at school, I became an easy target. The kids teased and bullied me, chasing me all the way home many afternoons and my classmates weren't my only tormentors. I vividly recall the humiliation I suffered at the hands of a Sunday school teacher who publicly shamed me for my limited reading skills. Her words crushed me as a child when she said publicly, "Boy, it's a shame you can't read!" I never went back.

As if this wasn't enough to endure, the emotional and

psychological suffering I experienced was further compounded by physical deprivation. I walked around with holes in the bottoms of my socks and shoes, so my feet were always cold on rainy Tennessee winter days. I rarely had a jacket to wear, and the few items of clothing I did possess were usually filthy because we couldn't afford to pay for hot water and electricity. Often, I went to bed cold and hungry unless I managed to steal food from the local market.

However, hunger breeds ingenuity. I became a frequent visitor at the neighbor's house, typically around dinnertime, hoping they would offer me something to eat. Sometimes the neighbor, a single mother of limited means, told me, "It's time for you to go home!" I interpreted all of this to mean that there wasn't enough—enough food, enough resources, enough love—to go around. For years, I carried this message into my life, assuming that there would never be enough. I developed an assumption of lack, a "scarcity consciousness."

One day, when I was seven, as loud growls erupted from my stomach, I came up with a plan to redeem recyclable bottles at the neighborhood market, which I had seen done by some older kids. I still recall the excitement of anticipating buying chocolate chip cookies and a large cold grape soda. It was my first independent enterprise. I was prepared to venture out alone into the world, to stake my claim, snare my prize. However, on the way to the market, a young man blocked my path and took all of the bottles I had collected. I begged him to give them back, and he started to walk away.

I blindly followed him, and I suddenly found myself behind an old abandoned house near a bayou. At that moment, I realized he didn't want my bottles. He threatened to kill me if I didn't pull down my pants and touch my toes. Struck with fear, I began to cry and plead with him to let me go and return my bottles. The next thing I remember is picking up the bottles and walking home crying. I told my grandmother what happened, and she took me to the emergency room where a doctor confirmed I had been raped.

I had become a victim of a crime at seven years old. First, I had been emotionally brutalized by the abandonment of my parents, and now I was physically brutalized by a stranger. These traumatic events led me to believe I was not the cause of my reality, but a victim of my circumstances. I didn't feel like I belonged anywhere. Nowhere felt safe. I came to believe that to survive, I needed to be invisible, and I tried to make myself disappear. I was shy and withdrawn. I hoped no one would notice and hurt me.

When I was in middle school, I was already towering over my classmates because I had flunked two grades, and I couldn't blend in with the background anymore. Still, I attempted to become as small as I could by bending my knees when walking in line with the other kids. I rarely went outside to play because I knew I would be teased or bullied. Since I was told I could not learn, I never tried. I rarely bothered to set goals and the ones I did set required minimal effort.

For years, I wished that I could tear out the pages of my life and draft a new script. The universe owed me a do-over! I wished that I had parents who loved me. My grandmother died when I was eighteen, and I regretted that I had not told her before she passed, "I love you," and "Thank you for taking me into your home when no one else wanted me." I wished that I had stood my ground and said to the young man who raped me, "You have no power over me and you cannot destroy the fire within my soul because I will not be your victim!" I wished that I had said to my Sunday school teachers, "I am important. I am valuable. I am worthy of love and beauty, and nothing can change that. My worth is not defined by how well I read or a grade on a report card." But most of all, I wished that I had said to myself, "I love you just the way you are and I believe in you!" But I said nothing.

After years of exploring numerous spiritual traditions and practices, I understand now that I am the one who gets to ascribe a meaning to a particular event or circumstance in my life. I am the one who chooses how to interpret it, to minimize or maximize it, and whether to let it inspire or defeat me. Previously, I had kept reliving my past beliefs—defeatist negative ones—over and over again. After all, a belief is only a thought one keeps consistently thinking and recreating. Change your thoughts, change your beliefs, change your experiences.

Today, I realize that my beliefs were all a reflection of my self-perception. I had interpreted my parents not keeping me as abandonment, that since they apparently did not want me, I must be trash. I didn't consider that there might have been extenuating circumstances that made it impossible for them to keep me, or they might have thought they were giving me a better life by leaving me with my grandmother.

I blamed the people in my environment for my suffering. I hated myself for my lack of confidence and doubted that someone like me could ever be successful. I believed that people were always trying to take advantage of me, so I started allowing it. I wanted them to like or love me instead of hurting me. Of course, I would be proven wrong time and time again.

By the time I was eighteen, I hated the person I had become. I believed that I was weak and unintelligent, a failure. When I was angry, I would curse God and inflict physical pain on myself. I would rip my shirt, pound my chest, and slap my face to try to let out my anger. At least I no longer had to worry about others beating up on me. I was so used to being hurt that I became my own attacker. After middle school, my childhood tormentors had grown afraid of me, saying there was "death in my eyes."

release the old story

I am telling you about my childhood to paint a picture of where I came from. I'm here to tell you that, if I have been able to survive and thrive, as worthless as I felt, then you can too. I considered my childhood so embarrassing and shameful that I never thought I could overcome it. I couldn't get rid of the tarnish that I felt. I couldn't get my do-over. But what I didn't realize was that I didn't need a do-over; I was perfect the way I was. I just needed to realize that what I was believing was just a story, a bad fairy tale that I had made up.

For example, you can feel "certain" that you have to be a people pleaser to gain approval and life must be hard, but are these thoughts true? Everything we believe to be "true" is based on the norms and values of our families and the society in which we live. Our "truths" are based on the experiences we have had and what we have taken them to mean about ourselves and our lives. When something happens, it is just an event, it is neither negative or positive, but we immediately assign a polarity to it which then becomes part of our memory of what happened, and we continually reinforce it. We remind ourselves how "bad" we are and how "bad our lives are." In reality, whatever happened was just "what happened." It is our interpretation of what happened that we took to mean something and turned into false knowledge about ourselves.

These stories are completely made up. True knowledge comes from something beyond our physical reality; it comes from our higher selves, our direct knowledge of God. I had made up a very negative tale about myself. I saw everything from a very screwed up perceptual filter. I didn't see my beauty, joy, authenticity, talent as a speaker, or ability to reach people emotionally and spiritually; I had lost the connection to my heart and soul. I didn't see how loving or amazing I was.

When you tap into your higher self through meditation, prayer, and unconditional love, you become aware of the intuition, wisdom, and inner guidance that make everything possible. You create a vast expansive space in which to see the infinite possibility, maybe for the first time.

Albert Einstein said,

"Imagination is more important
than knowledge. For knowledge is
limited, whereas imagination embraces the
entire world, stimulating progress, giving
birth to evolution."

Your imagination, faith, and feelings make it possible for you to manifest your amazing future.

Matthew 17:20 reads, "Truly I tell you, if you have faith as small as a mustard seed, you can say to this mountain, 'Move from here to there,' and it will move. Nothing will be impossible for you." Faith is a feeling of confidence and trust that all things are possible, that you are inside of, and part of, infinite love. The only thing that is actually true about us all is that we are infinite love; the rest is a story we concocted.

When I released my sad old story, it changed my perspective. I became a conscious observer. I started to see the facts of my life without the perceptual overlay. I did not have a lot of money. Okay. My grandmother raised me. Okay. I stuttered as a child. Okay. I had issues reading and writing. Okay. I was pretty awesome! I just needed to rise to a higher level and look at my life through the eyes of love.

winning naturally

My message is that anything is possible when you are ready to shed your old story and see yourself as you truly are, divine love with unlimited potential. When you can harness all that you have including all of your unique gifts (and trust me they are substantial) you will be able to make your wildest dreams a reality.

I call this "winning naturally," and for me, it had nothing to do with growing up with or without a mother and father or having two arms, eyes, and legs. *Winning naturally* is the God-given ability of all people, our birthright. As we follow our calling and move by our faith, we win naturally.

As we look around the world, we see inventions that were created inside the minds of human beings like us. Almost everything that we see in this modern life—pictures, cars, works of art, electronics, the Internet, apps, computers, fashion, music, and books—all came from people's imaginations. In most spiritual traditions, it's believed that even the wonders of nature were first imagined in the mind of God before being manifested in the physical world!

All great technological and social advances are continuing to evolve every day from simple to more complex creations. The impossible is made possible when someone has determination and focuses on a vision instead of giving in to self-doubt, shame, or fear. We are the only ones who can choose what's possible or impossible for our lives. The choices we make now will determine our future realities. We have what we have today because of the choices we made yesterday!

> "You have powers you never dreamed of. You can do things you never thought you could do. There are no limitations in what you can do except the limitations of your own mind."
> *-Darwin P. Kingsley*

If we close ourselves off from possibilities, our lives will reflect unfulfilled dreams. But, if we open ourselves up to infinite possibilities, our lives may exceed our wildest dreams! I know mine has! As a child or even a young adult, I would never have imagined I would be a counselor, writer, author and, public speaker!

 **start fresh:**

If you truly believed that nothing could stand in your way, how would you show up differently? Close your eyes and imagine you are a new human being, just born, with no history. You are brand spanking new. You have no baggage, and nothing has happened to you, good or bad. You are simply *love*. You have not been defined. What could you do? Anything!

Consider these questions: How would you show up? How would you feel sitting, standing, walking, and breathing, knowing you can have and do anything that you want?

What kind of work ethic would you have on a joyful journey toward your goals? How would you be different in private or public situations if you knew you couldn't fail? And what is failure anyway? It doesn't exist. It's just another mental construct utterly dependent on your definition of success, fulfillment, and happiness.

describe how that would feel

dare to imagine... one GOAL

Play the mental and emotional imagination game. Use your five senses to visualize one thing you want to manifest down to the smallest detail. Feel it, see it, hear it, touch it, smell it, and taste it. Write down what you envisioned and the picture you painted with your words, exactly what you want to experience in this area of your life. Be open to your highest good and infinite possibilities. What is one area of your life that is a priority right now, a starting point?

How did it feel to visualize yourself as someone who is unstoppable? Getting a clear picture of where you want to be in your life and what you want to experience is a crucial first step in getting there. Otherwise, you'll never know in this lifetime what you are truly capable of achieving. Rather than being a self-directed force of nature, you will be more like a feather in a storm, blowing out of control and hoping that others will help you be safe and your dreams will magically manifest. By envisioning and making choices about what you want, you are putting directional energy into the universe so that it can assist you.

German philosopher Johann Wolfgang von Goethe said, "Whatever you can do, or dream you can do, begin it. Boldness has genius, power, and magic in it. Begin it now."

tell Spirit your plan

To start the process of creating your extraordinary new future, you just need to set an *intention*. An intention is an action statement that lets the universe know that you are going to do something, not that you merely *want* to do it. The first step in any plan is setting intentions.

For example, "It is my intention to finish my book by June first. It is my intention to write ten pages per night." When I have meetings with people, I like to set intentions. "It is my intention to listen with my whole being on all levels and hear any information Spirit has for me." Sometimes I tell my intention to the people I am coaching. It lets them know what I will be doing, and they often respond with their intentions. When we do things with intentionality, it means we are aware that we are moving in a particular direction. It focuses our energy.

what's your intention for change in your life? It is my intention to…

"I am willing to put myself through anything; temporary pain or discomfort means nothing to me as long as I can see that the experience will take me to a new level." – *Diana Nyad*

3

motivation

"If the only prayer you ever say in your entire life is thank you, it will be enough." -Meister Eckhart

When my grandmother died, the feelings of abandonment became even more exacerbated. I was at war with myself, and I experienced emotional pain and depression that wouldn't go away. I wanted somehow to make it stop. Death seemed to be the only way out.

The night of my grandmother's death, I grabbed a butcher's knife from the kitchen drawer and headed to my bedroom. I held up the knife samurai execution style and let the hate, rage, and sadness well up inside of me. As the tears flowed, my trembling hands tightened around the handle. I took a deep breath and closed my eyes. Just as I was about to plunge the nine-inch blade into my stomach, I detected a presence in one corner of the room. The energy grew bigger and brighter and began to embrace me, its warmth flooding my entire body, enveloping the whole room. I dropped the knife, fell into a fetal position, and cried myself into a deep sleep. I had wanted to die that night, but a presence so indescribably loving stopped me. It was a powerful reminder that I am unconditional, overwhelming love and I am important to the divine—my life matters.

> "I believe that you're great, that there's something magnificent about you. Regardless of what has happened to you in your life, regardless of how young or how old you think you might be, the moment you begin to think properly, there's something that is within you, there's power within you, that's greater than the world. It will begin to emerge. It will take over your life. It will feed you. It will clothe you. It will guide you, protect you, direct you, sustain your very existence, if you let it. Now, that is what I know for sure."
> *-Rev. Michael Beckwith*

After Spirit intervened in my life and thwarted my suicide attempt, my life suddenly become perfect—NOT! It was far from it. After my grandmother died, I was homeless for several years and couch and floor-surfed. I still felt as if I was taking up much-needed space and wanted to become smaller. Life had prepared me to survive on little food, clothing, education, hope, and love. But survive I would.

Cut ahead seven years. I had been staying with different friends and worn out my welcome. Everyone was kicking me out or making me feel unwanted. I didn't blame them; I was eating their food and taking up space in their homes. I tried sleeping in an old car I bought for $500, but the winters in Memphis could sometimes be below freezing. I was tired of living like this and couldn't take any more suffering. One morning at around three a.m., after not being able to sleep in my car and feeling exhausted and sorry for myself, I decided to drive to the edge of a cliff overlooking the Mississippi River. I stood outside the car and raised my fist to the sky. I cursed God and wanted to die. I yelled to the heavens and begged God to please take my life.

"I can't take any more feeling cold, unloved and helpless," I yelled. "Fuck you, God, I hate you! You did this to me! I didn't ask to come into this world. I've been good. I went to church every Sunday. I followed your commandments… I don't deserve this fucked up life. Please kill me!"

I stood there in the cold at the edge of the cliff sobbing, waiting for death, but nothing happened! I got back in my car, started the engine, and put my foot on the gas pedal, ready to put it in drive and speed over the cliff into the rocks and water below. Suddenly, as I was thinking about ending it all, I had a vision of my funeral and heard the voices of people I knew. They were saying things like: "I knew something was wrong with that boy;" "The boy needed help;" "He wasn't strong enough to handle this world;" "I feel sorry for him;" and "I wish that I could have helped him, but I was barely able to make it myself."

At that moment, an uncontrollable rage ignited in me. Instead of running from life, I decided to run towards it. If I was bold enough to curse the creator of the universe, then I was bold enough to take on anything life could bring my way, and I would be thankful for it. At that moment, I made a declaration to myself to never beg for bread again.

The next day, I filled out an application for a security guard position working the night shift. They hired me to guard construction sites, businesses, and parking lots which worked perfectly for me since I could stay in the guard shack with a heater every night and I had nowhere else to stay. Even though I wasn't supposed to sleep on the job, every evening I would have a nap.

I enrolled in Shelby State Community college in Memphis, where I received financial aid. I had an undecided major and took psychology and drama classes. I was even cast in a few plays. My guidance counselor told me that UPS was hiring students from school, and I got a job there. For the first time, I was able to get my own place (with a roommate). Homeless no more!

trying to thrive

Even though my life was looking up, and I finally had a place to lay my head, I was still in the survival mentality, and this instinct guided me to create a false image of myself. I was risk-averse, afraid to place myself in different situations or try new things because I didn't believe I could successfully perform. I would try to plan what I was going to say or do in advance so as not to embarrass myself. I was ashamed to read aloud, afraid others would detect weakness and ignorance in my stammering, stuttering, and mispronunciations. I was scared I would be found out. I was like a beggar in the street, only I was begging for love and approval. My solution was to try to look good in other people's eyes. I was convinced that if I had a nice body, a fast car, and stylish clothes, people wouldn't look down on me.

Everything I had observed seemed to prove this point. I learned at an early age that a well-dressed person was more respected and admired than a poorly dressed one. A person driving an expensive car received more positive attention than one who drove a jalopy, or no car at all. People with college degrees or titles, those with prestigious family lineages, and those who were famous were highly valued.

I lied to navigate my way into people's lives and ultimately win them over. I cheated on school exams and in romantic relationships. I stole. At the time, I thought I was the one doing the manipulating and using others to get what I wanted. Later, I discovered that I was the one being manipulated. It was all a façade. I had no real friends since all of my relationships were predicated on lies and inauthenticity. I was afraid that if people got to really know me, they would uncover my deeply rooted shame and self-hatred, they would discover that the only reason I was nice to them was that I wanted their praise, approval, and sympathy. I thought if they liked me, it would mean I was likable, if they thought I was successful, it would make me feel successful. I was wrong.

The insanity is that I was seeking the approval of people with their own insecurities and imperfections. It's as if there are two people in a sinking boat, neither of whom can swim. One begs the other, "Please save me!" I was hurt and judged by people who were also feeling hurt and judged. It was like I was a child again, back in Memphis, hoping my friend's mom would give me dinner when she didn't even have food for her own kids. I thought I had escaped that or was escaping it, but I was still doing it, putting my care and feeding emotionally in other people's hands, others as lost as me.

> "The need for change bulldozed a road down the center of my mind."
> -*Maya Angelou*

everyone is doing the best they can

At one point, I had a realization that everyone was always doing their best. I was doing my best, and the people around me were doing theirs. When people aren't having their basic needs like food, shelter, and clothing (not to mention love) met, they can't rise higher; they get stuck in the muck of just trying to survive. This is where I was: deep in the muck.

the turning point - acceptance

I started becoming aware of the winner within me when I stopped seeing myself as a victim and started accepting my situation. Acceptance is different from resignation; it is deeply understanding that something is as it is, and even going a step further and getting that "this is all FOR me." Everything that is happening was for my benefit. The universe is a masterful creator and has a plan. It works on our behalf. Paulo Coehlo said, in *The Alchemist*,

> "When you want something, all the universe conspires in helping you to achieve it."

Once I had this revelation, I knew I had to be the co-conductor (with Spirit) of my own life. Since I wasn't sure where to start, I began with what I loved—nature. I wanted to take in all that was beautiful, alive, and vibrant. Nature represented peace for me. It had never abandoned me or caused me to go hungry. It had never teased me or beat me up. I had never blamed it for my painful childhood or my insecurities. I had never accused it of harming me. I did not feel a need to seek approval from it, nor did it seem to need approval from me. We were good.

My appreciation process began with love. I would affix my gaze on a beautiful flower and carefully observe it as it slowly opened up to the world. I noticed that the longer I held it in awe, the more love energy I felt. I would then let my attention wander to a tree, transfixed by the movement of a gentle breeze blowing through its leaves and melodious birds singing their praises upon the branches. The longer I chose to appreciate the majestic tree—the power and strength of its trunk, the grace of its perched visitors—the better I felt. My core felt empowered. I became rooted like the tree.

appreciation

I quickly realized that the more I practiced appreciation, the more love welled up inside of me, and the more I found to appreciate. I began to notice how a single blade of grass doesn't need to compete for attention with the field. It recognizes it has a purpose of its own. In my apartment in the morning, I honed in on the sunbeams shining through the windowpane as they cast reflections on the pillows, walls, and floor. At night, I focused on the moonlight and a bright, distant star.

The results were immediate. My appreciation began to expand to everything and everyone around me. My relationships improved dramatically without any effort on my part. It felt natural to be in harmony with everyone. It was as if I was a giant magnet that had become irresistible because I was doling out so much love and joy. It is impossible to give appreciation without feeling the uplifting results within oneself.

The truth is that every circumstance and situation that you face is an opportunity to move you toward your goals and help you realize your dreams. Disappointment, depression, betrayal, abandonment, addiction, illness, and failure are all opportunities for the advancement and the expansion of your ideal self. Contrary to how it may feel, the hardships that you faced didn't come to break you down but to create an opportunity for you to break through. Obstacles provide seeds of transformation, critical openings inside your heart and mind through which you can realize the strength that dwells at the core of your being.

The thirteenth-century Persian poet Rumi said,

"The wound is the place where the light enters you."

If you give up in the face of adversity or give in to fear and doubt, you may miss out on an opportunity to grow stronger and become fully aware of the master within yourself. Challenging situations and circumstances have no real power over you but these moments provide incredible opportunities to use your power of choice to turn disappointment into victory, depression into joy, betrayal into love, abandonment into strength, sickness into health and failures into motivation for success. Opportunities don't happen by chance or luck; you create them with your enthusiastic preparation. An aware person takes a loss and turns it into a win. Failure and mistakes are tools that force us to reevaluate our lives and wake us up to the love and success that we are made for and, in fact, already are.

redefine what has happened

For me, a transformation occurred when I realized that all of the experiences I had during my life made me more accessible to the suffering of others. I could uniquely relate to those who had gone through similar situations and have been a beacon to help them through their own storms. If I hadn't experienced life, I wouldn't have had much to say. This insight provided me with a powerful new way to look at everything that had happened to me, a way to redefine my past. My experiences have given me leverage into relating authentically and intimately with others. I can speak to painful experiences that others have had because I have "been there and done that." My past has served me well.

☆ Viola Davis

Viola Davis was born in St. Matthews, South Carolina on her grandmother's farm, a former Singleton Plantation in a one-room shack. She described her childhood.

"[There was] no running water. No
bathroom. It's just an outhouse. But my mom
says that the day I was born, all of my aunts
and uncles were in the house, everyone was
drinking and laughing, and having fun. She
said she ate a sardine, mustard, onion, tomato
sandwich after I was born...
I love that story."

An actress and producer, Viola Davis is the only black woman to be nominated for three Academy Awards and to win one. She was the only black actress or actor to win the Triple Crown of Acting and was listed by *Time Magazine* as one of the 100 most influential people in the world. Even though she grew up in abject poverty, living in condemned rat-infested buildings when she was a child, she was able to rise above her past and create an amazing future. After attending high school, Viola studied theater at Rhode Island College and attended the world-renowned Juilliard School. She broke into acting with the role of a nurse in *The Substance of Fire*. Since that time, she has been in dozens of movies and is considered one of the most talented actresses of all time.

Viola is an example of an amazing woman who didn't buy into stories of limitation and poverty. She "allowed" herself to have an amazing, successful career.

practice acceptance

What are some experiences that have happened in your life that you haven't been able to accept? Remember, you don't have to like or agree with them to accept them. You are just acknowledging that they are what they are.

List out some things you haven't been able to accept in the past. Then write, "I am accepting... (xyz experience)."

 **redefine experiences in your life**

What are some of the situations or experiences in your life that you have let define you? *(i.e. My parents gave me to the care of my grandmother.)*

How did you define that? (i.e. My parents abandoned me.)

Is there a way you can redefine this to be more supportive or positive for you? (i.e. My parents were too young to care for me so I was given a better opportunity in life with a loving relative.)

Are there more experiences? Use additional paper if necessary and repeat these questions.

 make these quotes your own

Apply these quotes to your personal life to make them your own and repeat them daily as affirmations.

Quote:

"I spend one hundred percent of my time focusing on the opportunities of today rather than the problems of yesterday."
- M. Dyer

Personalization:

"I will spend one hundred percent on my time on practicing the violin for one hour rather than criticizing myself for how I performed yesterday."

Quote:

"In the middle of every difficulty lies opportunity."
- Albert Einstein

Personalization:

"In the middle of my difficulty with peer pressure lies the opportunity for me to focus on loving myself more."

Quotes to Personalize:

"Opportunity often comes disguised in the form of misfortune, or temporary defeat." - Napoleon Hill

"Take the opportunity right now to seize the moment."
- M. Dyer

"Opportunity does not knock, it presents itself when you beat down the door." - Kyle Chandler

"Healing is a matter of time, but it is sometimes also a matter of opportunity." - Hippocrates

"If you don't like something, change it. If you can't change it, change your attitude." - Maya Angelou

what are your opportunities/dreams?

Make a list of opportunities you have right now in your life by area. Below are several common life areas (others may include children, parents, hobbies, travel or pets).

Relationship/partner:

1.

2.

3.

4.

Job/Finances:

1.

2.

3.

4.

House/Apartment/Living Situation:

1.

2.

3.

4.

Education/Training:

1.

2.

3.

4.

Health:

1.

2.

3.

4.

Friendships:

1.

2.

3.

4.

Service:

1.

2.

3.

4.

Spiritual Practice:

1.

2.

3.

4.

Other:

1.

2.

3.

4.

 redefine it all {on paper}

Is there a situation in your life that is bothering you right now? Take out a piece of paper and write it down. What happened? What did you do? Was there someone else involved? What did they do? How did you react? In hindsight (or higher sight), is there another way you could view the situation? This process is called *redefining,* changing the way you hold something within your consciousness so that it is more supportive and positive. It's a way of looking at life with a "glass half-full" approach.

practice gratitude

What are some things you are grateful for?

"You are today where your thoughts have brought you; you will be tomorrow where your thoughts take you."
-*James Alle*

4

falling In love

"Your task is not to seek for love, but merely to seek and find all the barriers within yourself that you have built against it." -Rumi

The feeling of love is not like a bachelor's degree you earn and then hang on the wall and pat yourself on the back for achieving; it requires continual awareness.

We are love, but we don't see it. Once we realize that we are love and we don't have to DO anything (other than seeing it in ourselves) the game is up—we have arrived!

In my own journey, my deeply rooted fear, shame, and insecurity led me to look outside of myself for love and approval. I believed that I was ugly, unworthy, and unsuccessful. I had never felt free to be my authentic, unapologetic self. In turn, my life had always been a reflection of my unworthy self-talk. I was afraid to ask for what I wanted and needed, believing that I would be rejected. I never seemed able to achieve what I wanted, to truly love and be loved, to even be happy. I was a player on a stage in constant need of applause. Once the lights were turned up and the patrons filed out of the theater, I was left alone gazing out into a sea of empty seats.

When I was in my mid-twenties, I fell so deeply in love with a woman that I did everything I thought she wanted to win her love. Our love story began on a cold December Memphis night. It was a Friday, and I was meeting a buddy at the Peabody Hotel for a party. As I stepped into a crowded room with the music blasting, I saw beautiful women walking around and dancing, wearing skin-tight dresses that they had to keep adjusting as they inched up their thighs. Of these gorgeous women, I was drawn to one who stood out in the crowd. She had on a short black skirt and halter top that revealed a silver navel ring. As she walked past me, I couldn't help but say hello and introduce myself. She smiled at me and said, "Hi, I'm Sheryl." The rest is history.

The timing for me was great; she had just broken up with her boyfriend. The love connection was visceral. We felt that soul mate energy; out of all the people at the party that night, our hearts called out to each other. And as luck (or fate) would have it, a month later something happened that sped things up for us. Someone broke into her apartment while she was still in bed and hit her on the leg with a baseball bat. She screamed, her roommate came running to her room, and the intruder escaped out the window. Sheryl called the police, believing that her ex-boyfriend, who was a drug dealer, had put someone up to hurt her. So, I became her protector and moved her into my apartment the next day. I would take Sheryl to work and pick her up. I was ready to defend her from any attack. It was my first time living with a woman, and I loved it. We would take baths and enjoy passionate moments together. Waking up next to her every morning made me not want to get out bed.

Sheryl had a hard time walking because of her leg injury, so, when we would go to the park to hang out, I would carry her on my back. I loved every moment. She said I made her feel safe, but she didn't know that she made me feel strong. This was the first time I had fallen in love! We would study *A Course in Miracles* and pray together. She was my lover and best friend.

One evening, I shared with her that I wanted to move to Los Angeles, and she didn't hesitate to say, "Let's do it!" Three months later, we loaded up my Toyota Celica and moved. We found a one-bedroom apartment in Hollywood, and both started going on auditions. She took a job as a waitress and was a professional dancer. I had been modeling for several years and started modeling in LA, New York, and Washington, DC.

We had been together for about six months at this point, and I thought our relationship was solid. Sheryl got a job performing in Japan for five weeks, and I would call her to let her know how much I missed her. When I went on auditions, I would meet some of the most beautiful women in the world, but I wasn't tempted at all because I was so deeply in love with her. The women I met were lovely, but I thought she was so much more, that she was my soul mate. I could tell her anything without judgment.

When she got back from Japan, I knew something wasn't right. She didn't want me to touch her. Then, one night, I decided to surprise her like I used to. I hid behind the sofa and waited until she came into the apartment, but this time, the surprise was on me. Before I could jump up, I heard her pick up the phone and say to someone on the other end, "He's not here!" I guess the man on the other end of the phone must have asked her if she wanted him to come back and pick her up because she answered, "No, I can't wait to move out of here."

At that moment, my heart was broken. Everything I believed to be true felt like a lie. I wanted to stand up and show myself, but my whole body began to shake uncontrollably, and I couldn't catch my breath. My world got dark and cold. I got up, and Sheryl stood there shocked, with her mouth gaping open. She hung up the phone, and for a minute, I went crazy. I couldn't believe what was happening; it seemed surreal. Weeping, with a feeling of disbelief, I grabbed her and held her against the wall. How could the love of my life betray me? How could the woman I was willing to defend with my life do this to me?

A week later, she moved in with a girlfriend in North Hollywood. When she was gone, I would wake up in the middle of the night with tears running down my cheeks onto my pillow. There was a pain in my heart that wouldn't stop. I would try to go to the gym to workout, and tears would begin to fall. I would go to the grocery store and walk down the aisle where we shopped and start to cry. Nothing I did could stop the pain.

I told her that I wanted to see her and she agreed to meet me at seven in the evening. Where she was living was about half an hour away from me. I drove to her apartment at the meeting time, but she didn't come to the door, so I went all the way back home and called her again (we didn't have cell phones back then). She answered and said she hadn't heard the door so I went back again and she still didn't respond to my knocking. I returned to my apartment feeling hurt and angry, but I was not able to go to sleep, so I returned at five in the morning and parked my car outside of her apartment building. At seven a.m., she and a man started walking to the street holding hands, and I lost my mind! I got out of my car and walked over to them. Sheryl asked the man to leave, and I told her to get in the car and drove off quickly before she could get out. We ended up at my apartment, standing in the kitchen. Refusing to look at me, she said, "Take me home!"

As she begged me to take her back to her place, I stood there in silence as pain and rage washed over me. It suddenly hit me that she was never going to return to me and that there was nothing I could do to make her love me. I drove her back to her new man and never tried to contact her again. Still, I always wanted to call her. It pained me so much to imagine how happy she was without me. Night after night, as I cried myself to sleep, I prayed that the feeling of needing her love would leave me.

I realized that if it was real love, I would have wanted her to be happy unconditionally, even if it was not with me. True love is wanting the best and highest good for someone else and myself, it's about appreciation and not manipulation and control. I realized I had no idea what love was. I still thought that it was outside of myself. I wasn't in love with her but in desperate need of loving myself! As a result of this breakup, I started journaling and writing poetry. Here's one of the poems that came through.

Falling Leaves

Like a leaf falling from a tree,
I fell to my knees

She was the apple of my eye,
The sunshine of my darkest night
I knew she was the one
Because my heart said so
She was standing in the wind
With a beautiful golden glow
Her eyes were like rays of light
Penetrating my soul

Like a leaf falling from a tree,
I fell to my knees,

I knew our love was meant to be,
She was the one for me
A thousand years of loneliness
Her hand I would hold,
Her lips I would kiss.
I long to see her face and
Experience her embrace
To feel her voice blowing softly upon my ears
For it has been a thousand years
With no love in sight.
She would be the one
Who could turn my cold nights into
Warm summer days

With sprinkles of heaven on her wings,
We would fly away together in this liquid
Yellow, blue and purple light
But I am sad to say that day will
Never come my way
For she turned her light away from me
She said my love was too strong
And the love felt wrong,
That I moved too fast,
So the love would never last,
I couldn't hold back the feelings inside,
The words I could not hide.
They just rushed from lips
Like a great ocean tide
I could not deny that I needed her love

So, like a leaf falling from a tree
I fell to my knees
And cried, our love would never be.

what is the lesson?

When my umpteenth girlfriend left me, it should have
been a sign that there was something in me that I needed to
work on, and I did realize this, I just didn't know what it was.
I thought it was that I wasn't good enough or that I was too
clingy. This is how it seemed from my human perspective.
However, I wasn't looking at my pattern from a Spiritual
perspective. What did all of these relationships have in
common? Someone had "abandoned" me. And this wasn't

the first time in my life I had felt abandoned. My parents had abandoned me, and I had interpreted my grandmother's death when I was eighteen as abandonment. Collectively these experiences represented a pattern of abandonment. Why would I have this pattern? From a human perspective, it just seems like I was having bad luck, but from a higher perspective, it's quite different.

Why would I attract experiences in which women would come and abandon me? Why would I choose people that would do this? All experiences are provided to us for one reason only: learning. My soul had come in to heal a pattern of abandonment or to learn self-worth. How do I know this? If my soul had not come in to this lifetime to learn this, I wouldn't have attracted situations of abandonment and, if I did happen to have an experience of this, like parents leaving me when I was young, I might have chosen to see it through a different perceptual filter; I may have seen it as my loving parents giving me a better opportunity in life for instance. But, because I came in with a particular "lesson," until I healed the pattern, I would continue to attract people to fill that role and experience the lesson over and over again.

How did I attract these people to fill this role for me, to be my teachers? My attractor field was beaming out powerful energy into the universe, sending me people who had a complementary pattern to work on.

Not only was I transmitting to the universe that I needed people to leave me, but I was also broadcasting out my inner reality: my low self-esteem, feelings of unworthiness, and belief that I didn't have enough resources, and therefore, it gave me back those things. According to the *Spiritual Law of*

Reflection, I drew back to me people and situations that would reinforce these beliefs. It would send me women that treated me poorly, cheated on me, or didn't love me. It didn't send me money making opportunities but reinforced poverty and lack.

I abandoned me

The universe was also reflecting a pattern that I had been doing to myself: I had been abandoning myself. I wasn't loving myself. I didn't think I was worthy. The way out of this was to look for all the ways the pattern was playing out inside me. I had to work on loving me. I had to really know that *I am the love.* When you figure out that you are the love and that God created you in his image (if you believe in that) or you wouldn't have been born in the first place, then it's possible to release the negative misunderstandings about yourself. That's what they are—just misunderstandings. You started out as a cute, screaming, babbling baby, and then you "learned" that something was wrong with you—in my case my parents left me—and made a judgment about yourself. To undo this damage, you need to fix that judgment; reverse it.

There are several ways to undo this damage so you can release the story you have been telling yourself. The first step is getting in touch with the judgment that you made. State the judgment out loud, modifying it until it resonates inside. In my case, a judgment was, "I judged my parents as wrong for leaving me." Another was, "I judged myself unworthy of my parents' love." The antidote is realizing the judgment was in error and letting it go, allowing the misunderstanding to flow up into the cosmos and disappear. If you can go into your heart and really know that the beliefs were made in error and that you and everyone around you are perfect, then the judgments will disappear. They were built on an incorrect assumption, an unstable foundation. Just letting them go by rising higher than the consciousness in which the misunderstanding (judgment) resided is liberating. If you can't get above the misunderstanding, you can work the problem within your ego, at the level the judgment was created. To do this, practice forgiveness. Since judgment is an inside game, you need to forgive yourself.

For example: "I forgive myself for judging my parents as wrong for leaving me; they were doing the best they could."

"I forgive myself for judging myself as unworthy; I am a manifestation of God so, by my very nature and creation, I am worthy."

A third way to release all of the energy around the pattern is to bring tons of light to the situation. Close your eyes and try to get in touch with the time you first remember experiencing the pattern. In my case, this was when I felt the absence of my parents. I was a little boy. I felt scared and alone.

Go back into your heart and experience what it was like for that child. Tell the child, "I love you, and I am here for you. You are safe. I will take care of you. You are not alone. You are so wonderful and smart and amazing, and I love you so much. I will never abandon you." Talk to the younger being about whatever happened that created the misunderstanding and rooted the pattern and assure him or her that you are always going to be present as their protector.

your partner is your teacher

By releasing the pattern, you are cleaning up your attractor field. You are literally changing what is being broadcast out to the universe, and you can start to attract people who will reflect the "cleaned up" you! Of course, if you still have other patterns to work on, like self-love, courage, lack, etc., you will start to call in those people. But you can clean up those patterns too!

Wouldn't it be great to start attracting people and situations into your life that are more fun? You can. You just have to do the work! But the work can be done. Trust me, if I can do it, so can you. I had a huge pattern of insecurity and clinginess. I was desperate for the love I had never experienced, and I had built up romantic love to be the only thing that could "save me." At one point, I actually bought a diamond ring (yes, you heard me right) for a woman I hadn't even had a date with or been intimate with! Of course, she sent it back to me and didn't want to have anything to do with me. I wish I had just taken my time. But then again, she was responding to my casting call for someone to reject me, so our fate was sealed! Which brings me to relationships in general. What the heck do we have these relationships for in the first place?

Relationships are where we work out most of our issues in life. We pick partners who are complementary to us and I don't mean that they compliment us like, "Hey, you look gorgeous today," although that would be nice too. What I mean is that they are our complement; they have patterns that fit perfectly into our patterns. You may have the same pattern (i.e. both were abandoned, cheated on partners or were cheated on) or patterns that fit together like positive and negative (one cheated on partners and the other has been cheated on by partners). You pick someone who will be your teacher. If we are lucky and figure out that we should use everything as a learning opportunity, we can figure it out and start to have enjoyable, mutually loving and supportive relationships. If we don't get the message, we keep getting the same lesson but with different teachers. In my case, they were all beautiful women that left me. I was a slow learner. At least they were gorgeous, so I had fun along the way…for a while.

relationships are our schools for healing

Our partners are generally our biggest challengers because we love them, and we take what they say and do to heart. We are at our most vulnerable with them. And so many of us have misunderstandings about love that we learned from our parents and the media. We may confuse love with ownership. Our sexual feelings for another person also muddy the waters. It's important to remember that relationships are about "relating." They are just another form of love, and true authentic love is unconditional. It is not about games, betrayal, and worthiness. Those all come into play in romances at the ego level. True love is authentic. When we are really in love, we are "in" the "love" with another. True love is respectful, supportive, authentic, and unconditional.

How can you heal your relationships? One great way to start is to look for all the judgments you are placing on your partner (i.e. she is so self-centered). Clear those judgments of him or her by forgiving yourself. "I forgive myself for judging her as vain." Then, since the law of reflection says it is also happening inside you (since your outer perceptions are mirroring back perceptions that are within yourself), you can assume you are also judging yourself as those same qualities. In this example, you would be judging yourself as vain, so you would say, "I forgive myself for judging myself as vain." We may also judge someone for a quality they have as a negative or "bad" quality, a quality we don't have or understand ourselves. For example, I might have judged someone as "showing off" because of my lack of confidence, since I was too shy to "show off."

What are all the things that "bother" you about your partner? Make a list and clear them all. Clear each quality as it relates to your judgment of your partner and as if you were placing the same judgment on yourself. Often we are aware of judging something in another person that we don't realize we are also judging in ourselves. The ego doesn't like to judge itself consciously since it feels unsafe, so it just projects the judgment onto someone else, which feels safer. Just assume the judgment is also about yourself and say the self-forgiveness. You can see if it resonates. If it doesn't, ask your inner self to clarify the statement until it does.

Next, focus on the great qualities of your partner. Bring the light into your relationship.

look through the eyes of love

If you have an argument, ask yourself, "What is it about this situation that upsets me the most?" That is the key, where you have to do the work. For example, if you think, "It reminded me of how my ex-girlfriend treated me when she left me for my best friend; I felt insignificant and unworthy," then the key is to work on insignificance and unworthiness. When did you first experience these types of feelings? Follow the feelings back inside you to where you first started feeling them and heal the memories of the experiences (because they still feel real inside you).

In addition to doing the specific healing work at the ego level, you can rise above the ego to a higher consciousness level. Look at the situation through God's eyes (or whatever higher power you believe in). Look at the person as a soul having an ego experience. You can still love someone even if they are behaving in a way that you don't like. I always try to see people as doing the best they can. It helps me to give them the respect they deserve and the benefit of the doubt. When I look at someone as a soul, or I see into their soul, I feel less affected by whatever part they are playing in any drama that is going on. I can step outside of myself and see what is actually happening: a person in front of me is in upset.

As Miguel Ruiz says in his book *The Four Agreements,* "Don't take anything personally." When you look at everything through the eyes of love, animosity disappears. When there is true authentic love, hatred, and negativity dissolve; they can't co-exist.

It isn't personal ever. Don't take it that way. People are going through their own drama. You may contribute by being negative or by some way you are behaving, but it is not about you. Relationships feel VERY personal because they can hurt so much.

heart-gazing

A way to connect with your heart and that of another is through heart-gazing. It is a state of being totally present with yourself or another person without judgment. To do this, tune into to your heart by looking in a mirror or thinking of a person or animal you love unconditionally. Stand close to the person you are heart-gazing with and look into each other's eyes until you can see your reflection in them. Do this for three to five minutes. Don't have anyone to heart-gaze with? You can also use a picture of a loved one or the cover of this book since it's infused with my soul essence.

It may not be easy. When I first practiced soul gazing with myself and others, it was uncomfortable because we aren't taught to be vulnerable ourselves or be around other's vulnerability. Most people aren't comfortable making eye contact. We aren't used to being around other's issues and silence without trying to fix them or fill the silence. Often when I'm working with a client, I give them a mirror and have them look into their own eyes with love and appreciation. If they can't access their emotions, I suggest they think of someone they love unconditionally. Once they are feeling emotion, it's usually easier to send themselves love and gratitude. I have found that this practice is especially useful with couples and families.

 heal an argument or misunderstanding

Identify a situation that happened recently in which you found yourself reacting negatively or with anger or sadness.

What happened?

What about this situation upset me the most?

What emotion(s) came up in me?

When have I felt that feeling before?

Can I forgive myself for feeling that way? I forgive myself for judging myself as...

do forgiveness work {on paper}

Identify judgments you have placed against your partner and do the forgiveness work. Forgive yourself for judging your partner for each thing, and forgive yourself for judging yourself for each of the same attributes/behaviors. Remember, judgment is an inside job—we are only responsible for ourselves, so we forgive ourselves only.

On a piece of paper, write "Judgments about my partner" and list them out. Then f*or each judgment, fill in the following four statements:*

1. I forgive myself for judging my PARTNER as:

2. The truth is:

3. I forgive myself for judging MYSELF as:

4. The truth is:

 (repeat for all judgments)

what do you love about your partner? (tell them!)

what do you love about yourself?

5

the journey

"We had thought that we were human beings making a spiritual journey; it may be truer to say that we are spiritual beings making a human journey." - Pierre Teilhard de Chardin

How did I begin my spiritual journey? It started when I was twelve when my Big Mama, as I called my grandmother, made arrangements for me to go to Benton County Mississippi to the Union Hill Baptist Church to have my soul saved, a tradition in her family for children when they reached their twelfth birthday. My uncle John drove us to my aunt's house where we would be staying since she lived near the church. It was like going back in time. My aunt lived in a two-bedroom white house next to a dirt road where every time a car drove by, it would leave a gigantic cloud of dust enveloping us. In front of the house was a water pump as well as two huge hogs and several piglets running around. There were no inside bathrooms, so we had to go out in the woods to do our business. Every morning for breakfast, I would have hot buttered biscuits made from scratch, bacon and eggs with fried potatoes, homemade strawberry, blackberry or peach jam, and molasses.

My cousin Cleveland, who was only 14 years old, drove us to the church that evening. It was a small one-room church; it only held about thirty people. There were seven of us kids, and we all had to go sit in the front row, on the "mourner's bench." The preacher, Reverend Gaston, was a tall, good looking man with gold in his mouth who would use a white handkerchief to wipe the sweat and spit from the side of his mouth as he spoke. He was so powerful that the women in the congregation couldn't control their bodies and would swing their arms, get out of their seats, and run up and down the aisles. With the Spirit in them, some would roll around on the floor. They would scream and shout, and some would repeatedly say, "Hallelujah! Thank you Jesus!" It was called "shouting" when the Holy Spirit would take over your body, and you would lose control; when God took possession of body and soul.

The revival, the process of saving my soul, would last seven days, from Sunday to Sunday. Each day, we were given a prayer to repeat over and over again: "Lord Have Mercy on My Soul!" Since I was told this was best done out in the woods alone, I went out in the woods and prayed for hours every day. I remember being terrified I might run into a snake or whatever else might be in the forest, but I did it anyway because I wanted God to save me, to go to heaven when I died, for God to protect me. Each evening I went back to the church and sat on the mourner's bench, praying God would save my soul, and each night other kids were being saved as the Reverend Gaston gave his powerful sermons.

I still remember many of them. The first night was Matthew 17:20 "And Jesus said unto them, Because of your unbelief: for verily I say unto you, If ye have faith as a grain of mustard seed, ye shall say unto this mountain, Remove hence to yonder place; and it shall remove..." Two kids rose up with the power of God in them and were saved that night.

On Monday, there was another powerful sermon, and one child got saved; on Tuesday night, two more. By Wednesday night, I was praying hard to get my soul saved. I was one of only two kids left on the mourning bench, waiting to be saved.

The preacher's booming voice filled the church, "As the Father has loved me, so have I loved you. Abide in my love. If you keep my commandments, you will abide in my love..."

As I was listening, the person to the right of me was getting up. Then I felt Spirit take control of my heart, body, and mind. I had been praying hard, and the Reverend Gaston was on fire that night. The room was filled with light, and I was crying with joy. I got up and started to walk toward the pulpit. I was moving back and forth as if I was intoxicated. I *was* intoxicated, filled with the love of the Lord. Reverend Gaston's words of God pierced my heart, as God came and awakened my soul. Hallelujah!

anger everywhere

Fast forward about fifteen years, and I was on a fresh spiritual journey. I needed some answers. My latest relationship had crashed and burned, and I realized that I was the common factor in all of my relationships. I wanted answers, so I became a spiritual student. I turned to *A Course in Miracles*, Tony Robbins, Abraham Hicks, Wayne Dyer, Deepak Chopra, and Agape Church. I read dozens of books, but I couldn't get rid of the shame I felt. I thought, "The only thing left to do is to kill you, shame. None of these self-help gurus can save your life." I had to end the pain, shame, and insane thoughts.

So I decided to have a conversation with shame. I closed my eyes and asked "shame" to come forward. It said to me, "The teachers said you should be ashamed because you couldn't read. But you've always been stupid." I told the shame, "You were never stupid." It said, "It was your fault, you let that boy hurt you. You let it happen. You should have run. You are damaged. If you couldn't even trust yourself to escape, then, how can you trust yourself in life now?"

I responded, "We were just a little boy. We didn't know better. We didn't know what was going to happen."

Shame said, "It's not just me in here. You also got to worry about anger."

So next, I called forth anger and asked it what it wanted to tell me.

Anger said, "You aren't as nice as you are portraying to the world. You are a fraud. You have always been a fraud."

What anger was saying was true: everyone thought I was so nice, but I had a dark side. When I was young, I used to get into fights with all the basketball players; they called me "killer." My best friend would beg me to stop fighting with the kids because he just wanted to get on with the game. I fought almost every day. Once, as a young adult, I kicked my girlfriend's door down because I thought she had a man hiding in her apartment. It turns out she did have someone hiding in her apartment, but it was a girlfriend of hers, buck naked in the closet. That was a shock. At that point, I only wished I'd come in sooner and been invited to the party!

But seriously, what was I thinking? Why did I think it was okay to break her door down? These were the questions I started to ask myself. Why was I so angry?

I kept talking with anger. I knew from all my spiritual studies that underneath anger is always hurt, so I wanted to clear this up. Going through life with this anger inside myself felt awful; it was causing me to suffer. I had to get rid of it if I was going to continue living and have a happy life.

Anger was pretty pissed off at me for "forcing" my parents to leave when I was little. Apparently, it was all my fault. It wasn't surprising that my anger told me this since it's quite a common misunderstanding. Often children think it is their fault when a parent leaves. So I apologized to anger and said it was a misunderstanding and that it was okay to be angry. Anger was expressing that it was hard being poor and hungry all those years. I said I understood. When about a half hour had passed, anger just burst into tears. Sadness is always underneath anger, and sadness wanted his say. He missed mom and dad. "Why wasn't he enough?" I comforted him and told him I love him. I wrapped my arms around myself and told myself, "I love you" and, for the first time, I really meant it.

take responsibility

I took responsibility for my feelings. I had conversations with my shame, anger, and sadness and tried to clear up old assumptions I had made when I was a child. While I wasn't responsible for the abuse I had suffered, I was responsible for how I had internalized it. I wanted to take dominion over my feelings so I wouldn't take them out on myself or others anymore. Until we take full responsibility for how we have acted and where those actions have taken us, we can't manifest something else. Until we say, "My actions and beliefs got me here," we can't improve our lives. We will be stuck. As long as we are victims—so and so did this to me and poor me—we can't move up. We will be like Einstein's definition of insanity: doing the same thing over and over again and expecting different results. Once we take complete dominion over ourselves, we can change our stories.

> ## "Taking responsibility means not blaming yourself."
> ### -Susan Jeffers

Once we take responsibility, we can examine our decisions. In any given situation, there are many different types of choices we can make, both inner and outer. For example, when my girlfriend left me, after a critical period of mourning, I could have chosen to think that it was for my highest good because she wasn't the right person for me. I could have reflected on the idea that when "God closes a window, he opens infinite doors," or to look at it as an opportunity to examine my blocks against love. I could have reflected on how I might behave differently in relationships in the future. I might have chosen to believe that the relationship ending gave me more time to focus on other areas of my life. It's all about how we see what has happened. Everything that happens is FOR us. As long as we use our choice to see life in this way, we can create anything!

> "You may believe that you are responsible for what you do, but not for what you think. The truth is that you are responsible for what you think because it is only at this level that you can exercise choice. What you do comes from what you think."
> —*Marianne Williamson, Reflections on the Principles of A Course in Miracles*

⭐ Maya Angelou

What an inspiration! Born "Marguerite Annie Johnson" in 1928, Maya Angelou is a poet laureate, Pulitzer prize nominee, Tony Award winner, best-selling author, poetess, winner of more than fifty honorary degrees, mother, sister, daughter, wife, National Medal of Arts winner, Presidential Medal of Freedom winner, consummate and powerful woman, and artist. Angelou took her difficult past and turned it into extraordinarily moving poetry and prose.

At the age of eight, while living with her mother, Angelou was sexually abused and raped by her mother's boyfriend, who was jailed for only one day and then released! Four days later he was murdered, presumably by one of her uncles, and she became mute for five years. She thought her voice had killed the man since she had spoken his name! Angelou credits a teacher and friend of her family, Mrs. Bertha Flowers, with helping her speak again by introducing her to literary masters and black female artists like Frances Harper, Anne Spencer, and Jessie Fauset.

Over her lifetime, Maya Angelou worked as a streetcar conductor, cocktail waitress, cook, dancer, prostitute, and madam. She stated, "There are many ways to prostitute one's self," and she was never ashamed. Angelou says,

> "I wrote about my experiences
> because I thought too many
> people tell young folks,
> *'I never did anything wrong. Who, moi?*
> *Never I. I have no skeletons in my closet.*
> *In fact, I have no closet...'*
> They lie like that and then young
> people find themselves in
> situations and they think,
> *'Damn, I must be a pretty bad guy.*
> *My mom or dad never did anything wrong.'*
> They can't forgive themselves and
> go on with their lives."

When you say Maya Angelou's name to people, they often remember her famous autobiography, *I Know Why the Caged Bird Sings,* her voice and kindness when she spoke, or her dozens of beautiful, inspiring poems including *Phenomenal Woman, On the Pulse of Morning*, and *Still I Rise.*

how does taking responsibility affect YOUR life?

Learning to take full responsibility releases us from any victimhood we may be experiencing. We make choices every day that directly or indirectly impact what happens to us. What are some choices you made that you could re-think?

A choice I made:

What are some different choices I could have made in this situation?

Could I have chosen to look at something differently or responded differently?

What are the *inner* choices that I made—how I chose to look at the situation? How could I choose to look at it differently, hold it within my consciousness more positively?

What are the *outer* choices that I made—are there things I said or did that weren't the most supportive choices? What could I have done differently?

Can I forgive myself for any lingering judgments I have about others or myself relating to this situation?
I forgive myself for judging myself as...
I forgive myself for judging xyz as...

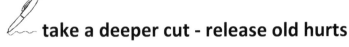 **take a deeper cut - release old hurts**

Make a list of all the judgments that you have placed on yourself and others. Be very thorough. Write them on a piece of paper so you can destroy them later. You don't want them permanently connected to you. Then forgive each one. You can read the list daily for a month and forgive each one in turn. Remember, you don't want to be a victim; no one did anything to you. If you had a judgment against another person (like your friend Carlos), say, "I forgive myself for judging Carlos as xyz."

Your paper would look like:

Judgment:

Forgiveness: *(Repeat)*

clear new judgments as they happen

Just as important as clearing up all the old stuff in our pasts, is clearing up new stuff as it comes up. Make a commitment to yourself to clear new judgments as they happen. How do we know when our consciousness is getting cluttered, when we have a judgment that has taken up residence? Whenever we say to someone, "I'm upset because" or "I'm mad (or sad) because" we are judging. Recently, when I was facilitating a life skills session in juvi, a teen said, "I'm upset because this kid disrespected my hood."

When he told me this, I could tell that one of his beliefs had been violated. It required a little probing. Why was it bothering him so much? The belief that it had violated was: "My hood represents my identity, so I am being disrespected." From there, he took it even deeper and realized that he didn't value himself, and he had been seeking outside validation. Since his parents hadn't seemed to respect or value him, the only value he had gotten was from his homies.

follow the feelings

A young woman, Marsia, told me that she was *upset because* her mother was criticizing her choice of a boyfriend, and had said, "Why are you hanging out with him? He dresses like a gangbanger and he doesn't respect you?"

Marsia was crying when she was describing it to me; she felt deeply hurt. Her mom was very critical of her, always putting her down for her choices. I asked her to describe the feeling, and she said, "I'm not good enough." I asked her when she had first had that feeling.

She replied, "When I was about ten years old, I wanted to be on American Idol, and I was singing for my mom, and she said, 'Girl you sound terrible.'"

The way to heal the hurt in the present is to go back to heal it in the past. Usually, present-day hurts are accessing material in our consciousness that is left over from the past, reactivating old wounds. For Marsia, the remedy was to send love back to the energy of her younger self and clear up any misinterpretations she made at that time. She had to tell herself that she loved herself and that it was all a misunderstanding. Then she did the forgiveness work. "I forgive myself for judging my mother for not loving me and criticizing me. I forgive myself for judging myself as always letting my mother down. I forgive myself for judging myself as a bad singer. I forgive myself for judging myself as not good enough and not capable of making wise decisions." Then comes the truth statements: "The truth is that my mother loved me the best way she knew. The truth is that my voice is beautiful! The truth is that my voice doesn't define me and doesn't matter. The truth is that I'm very capable."

A few days later, Marsia told me that she had called her mother and brought up the singing episode from her childhood. She said, "Remember when you told me my voice was awful," and her mom responded, "I couldn't have said that, I love your voice." Then thinking about it, her mom remembered the incident and that she had gotten laid off from her job that morning! She was just lashing out at her daughter because she was having a terrible day.

She said to Marsia, "I'm so sorry, Baby, I love you. I was probably just thinking about my own voice. I always wanted to be a singer and I thought I could never do it. Plus, I wanted you to focus on your education. It was my own insecurity. I had just lost my job and I didn't want you to ever have to worry about money like I had to. I love you so much." Finding out that her mother hadn't meant to criticize her voice and had her own insecurities and issues that day changed the way Marsia held the memory of the experience within herself, and magically her feelings about her voice dramatically improved.

Often, when past stories have been resolved inside of us, they resolve in the real world as well. as if by magic! Once the story is eliminated, it no longer influences our attractor field, and miraculously, the attractor field changes. Once the misinterpretation is cleared up and no longer has a charge on it, everyone who is responding to it—in Marsia's case, her mother—change their responses as well. Even if her mother did not change her critical behavior in the future, Marsia began to see it differently, through the eyes of love and it didn't continue to affect her in the same way.

Responsibility affirmations

Repeat these affirmations aloud and write your own.

I am responsible for my thoughts and choices.

I am responsible for my life and my reality.

I am responsible for my happiness.

I am responsible for my beliefs.

I am responsible for my perception.

I am responsible for my gifts and my future.

automatic writing {on paper}

After I had my conversation with shame, anger, and sadness, I did some "automatic writing" to clear out any remaining energy. Sit in a quiet, private place with a few sheets of notebook paper and allow your hand to scribble out whatever comes up. Don't judge or evaluate what you are writing. The goal is just to get whatever is inside you out. You can write for about a half hour (or as little as 5 minutes). Don't save what you write; destroy it by tearing it up and flushing it down the toilet, or burning. Whenever I am bothered by something, and I'm not sure what it is, I use automatic writing to try to clear it out. Whatever is in my unconscious or subconscious comes out for clearing.

6

ten days in the desert

"All that we are is the result of what we have thought: it is founded on our thoughts and made up of our thoughts. If a man speaks or acts with an evil thought, suffering follows him as the wheel follows the hoof of the beast that draws the wagon...If a man speaks or acts with a good thought, happiness follows him like a shadow that never leaves him." - Gautama Buddha

How did I go from working part-time at UPS with my first apartment after being homeless, to being the person I am today? I went back to my essence. I cleared all of the misperceptions of myself and started fresh. I began to see myself as divine, to know that we are all divine.

In my early thirties, I had exhausted all of my options. I had studied Kabbalah, A Course in Miracles, Christianity, and every self-help book I could get my hands on, and my life was still a mess. My outer reality was mirroring back my inside world. I didn't know how to conquer my negative self-image, and so I was experiencing a negative outer reality. I was broke. I thought I needed a more secure job, so I gave up on modeling and acting, but my "secure job" wasn't that secure after all. I got a job as a massage therapist, but the hours and pay were terrible. Plus, it took a toll on my back and my wrists. My relationship was also on its way out.

Then, one night, a friend invited me to a get-together and two women were talking about an amazing retreat they went on, Vipassana, in which they spent ten days meditating in the desert. Being silent for ten days had brought them so much peace.

At this point in my life, I thought, "This is for me." But at the same time, I was a bit intimidated. It seemed intense. I didn't know if I could do anything like that. I started to make excuses for myself. "I can't afford it." But no! It was free, so I couldn't use that excuse! Spirit was removing all the barriers.

But since I didn't have a job anymore (I had just gotten fired) or a relationship (my girlfriend had just left me), I thought, "What the heck, I'm going!" And trust me, I was terrified. The last place I wanted to look was inside myself! Who knew what I would find? I had spent my life looking outside myself, so maybe it was time to look within instead.

I filled out the application online to go on the next retreat, which was about to begin in a few days, but they said they were full, and they would put me on the waiting list.

I thought, "Ok. They're full. I'm off the hook." I breathed a sigh of relief. But then, I was a bit sad. And, boom, the phone rang. Someone had just dropped out. So I packed my bags and loaded my old Volvo to make the five-hour drive.

what I learned meditating for ten days

I discovered I had a constant dialogue going on in my mind. My inner chatter wouldn't stop no matter how hard I tried to focus on my breath. We started meditating around four in the morning and continued until nine p.m.! There were food and bathroom breaks, but we didn't interact with any of the other participants. The first few days were about focusing on the breath, and the next few were about focusing on the body. On the first day, several people dropped out and ran away. I wanted to run too, but I stuck with it. One night, I broke the rules. I snuck off to sit in my car. I listened to my phone messages. I just wanted to hear voices.

I had visions. In one of my dreams, a woman was sitting on my bed naked with her back to me, and she turned her head to look at me. She had a tattoo of a star on her left shoulder that seemed so real. I had many realizations. One was that the mind is obsessed with the past and the future. My mind took me on a rollercoaster ride. I recognized that it wasn't giving me positive affirmations; it was critical. It was attacking me and holding me back, derailing every choice. It hated me. It despised me. It wanted me dead.

The voice told me I was wasting my time doing this "meditation stuff" and that I would die alone in an elderly home for the poor. The voice made me cry, and that was when I realized that there were different aspects of myself. There was a part of me that was speaking, a part of me that was listening, and a part of me that was observing the conversation. I was conscious that part of me was aware that it was taking place. I asked that voice, "Why are you saying this to me? Why would you attack me? Why would I hurt myself?"

I started to think about all those times I had wanted to end my life and all the negative judgments I had about myself. I realized at that moment that it must be an illusion because I thought, "How is it possible to hate myself when I am the self that is doing the hating? How can I be the giver and the receiver at the same time?"

I started to think about all the times I had wanted to end my life, all the negative conversations I had with myself about myself. I realized at that moment that this must be an allusion because, otherwise, it wouldn't have been possible for me to hate myself when I was the self that was doing the hating. I understood the concept of hating something outside of myself, like certain foods, the weather, or even another person. To hate, or love, something or someone you have to judge it or him/her.

Does a tree judge? Does a dog judge? Does the sun judge? I realized that I was experiencing insane thoughts: thoughts about separation and duality. I realized that in order for me to judge myself, there must be something in me experiencing separation from myself.

I once observed a man talking to himself and thought, "For him to be having a conversation with himself, he must be both listening to himself and responding to himself." This concept of duality within applied to my suicidal inclination as well. I hated myself but recognized that to hate myself, I had to see myself as both a victim and an assailant. I would be the murderer and the person being murdered. I often experienced conflict within. I would set goals and expectations for myself and then let myself down. I would also occasionally make myself proud, and it would mean I had done something to make myself proud. I was the person making myself proud and the person being proud. These observations gave me the knowledge that I was multi-dimensional in consciousness, which meant to me that, at any given time, a negative or positive thought could make choices using my body.

Have you ever been doing something and asked yourself, "Why did I do that?" Have you ever driven your car and missed the exit because your mind was somewhere else? If your mind was elsewhere, who was driving the car? Have you ever ended up somewhere you didn't want to be and yet along the way you made choices that got you there? I know this may sound philosophical to you but, remember, I was having these thoughts and insights during a ten-day silent meditation. I may have been in hour 160 by this time!

When I came back from the retreat, I had a new found sense of calm. I remember my ex-girlfriend screaming at me, and I did not react because I had no negative energy inside of me. I had no button that could be pushed. I was high for nine months! And I got a lot of stuff done! My life was really coming together. I had a peace about me. People would notice it and ask me, "What have you been doing?"

On the tenth month, life crept back in. I had started the fire, but I didn't fan the flame—I didn't do the follow-up work. I wish I had added on some spiritual exercises like automatic writing to clear some of the negative judgments I had about myself, or daily meditation. I needed to go deeper to stay deeper. My solution? I went back to the retreat every year for four more years. I did four more ten-day meditations over the next several years. Each time, I went deeper and deeper and would have more conversations with God. The last time during my mediation, I asked myself, "What is your purpose?" And Spirit answered me that my purpose is to help people see their potential. Once I knew my purpose and that I was here for a purpose, everything shifted for me. The old story disappeared (nearly) for good. Occasionally I would still have a negative thought, but at that point, I was able to just observe it and not let it take hold of me.

☆ Rick Warren

About this time, I saw an inspirational TED talk with Rick Warren, founder of Saddleback Church, who wrote one of the best-selling books of all time, *A Purpose Driven Life*.

He talks about God's question to Moses in Exodus 4:2, "What's in your hand?" He is referring to the staff that is in Moses' hand because he is a sheepherder, which represents what Moses has at his disposal. He is making a point that it is our life's work to figure out what we are here for and what tools we have in our hands. Whatever is in our hand exemplifies our identity, income, and influence. If we have a pen in our hand, our gift may be writing. Warren said,

> "If you will take it and give it to Jesus
> he will make it come alive.
> He will do things in your life you would
> never imagine."

what is your shape?

Rick Warren uses the acronym SHAPE to stand for the qualities that you possess that make you unique and determine what your gift to the world may be: your Spiritual gifts, Heart, Abilities, Personality, and Experiences. What do you have going for you? He says,

> "When you use your SHAPE and you do what God made you to do, it not only feels good, but it also makes God smile. You know what makes God smile? When he looks down and sees you and me using the talents that he gave us for his glory."

Rick Warren is a great role model. Not only are his talks incredibly inspirational, but he gave away virtually all of the proceeds from the sale of his best-selling book, millions of dollars, to foundations and causes to help those in need.

what are your special blessings and talents? What is unique about you?

What are you blessed with? (i.e. I'm blessed with charisma)

What have you always felt called to do? (i.e. I've always wanted to work with kids)

What are your skills? (i.e. I know how to write)

What are your personality traits? (i.e. I'm outgoing/likable)

What is your background? (i.e. I understand poverty)

☆ Annie Sullivan

There are many examples in history of people who recognized and utilized their unique qualities and gifts to help others. Annie Sullivan's family emigrated from Ireland to Massachusetts when she was young during the great famine and, when she was small, her mother died, and her father abandoned her and her brother Jimmie at a filthy almshouse where her brother died within a few months. Annie went nearly blind and eventually, she was able to convince an inspector to admit her to the Perkins School for the Blind.

When she was twenty-one years old, she was hired by a family to teach their seven-year-old blind, deaf, and mute daughter Helen, and the rest is history. We've probably all seen it in the movie dramatizations of Helen Keller. Annie was the perfect person to teach and help Helen. What was in her hand? Blindness and a lot of love, toughness, and compassion. She was the perfect vehicle to help Helen learn to make sense of language and understand love. She assisted and loved Helen throughout her life, remaining by her side as Helen wrote books and even received a degree from Radcliffe College. To this day, Annie Sullivan and Helen Keller remain perhaps the most powerful examples of what is truly possible. If Helen Keller can do it, I can do it!

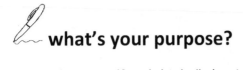

what's your purpose?

Go inside yourself and think, "what is my purpose?" If money wasn't involved and you could do ABSOLUTELY anything what might it be?

7

readiness

"If it be now, 'tis not to come. If it be not to come, it will be now. If it be not now, yet it will come—the readiness is all."
-William Shakespeare

Have you heard the one about the rabbit, the raccoon, the Billy goat, and the squirrel? The squirrel got word that a great winter storm was coming. She asked her friends if they'd be willing to help gather the food and provisions they'd need to get through the storm. But the rabbit, raccoon, and Billy goat said, "Sorry, squirrel! We've already made plans today. We're going to hang out by the lake and play video games. Then tonight, we're going back to raccoon's house to binge-watch *Game of Thrones*. We're much too busy to go out gathering nuts, berries, and sticks!"

The squirrel was ready to go out alone to gather nuts, berries, and sticks. When she was done, she asked her friends if they'd be willing to help build a shed to store the food. Again, they said, "No, we're too busy right now eating berries by the lake." So the squirrel had the willingness to built the shed and stored the food herself. Then the storm came. The driving winds and freezing rains blew through the forest, covering the plants and trees in a thick layer of frost. There was no food anywhere to be found. The rabbit, raccoon and Billy goat raced to the squirrel and said, "We know we weren't here before to help you find or store your food, but we're all willing to help you eat the food now!"

The squirrel looked at her friends and said, "You got to be kidding me!" Then she closed the door to her shed, thinking to herself, "I've got to get some new friends."

Even though we may not want to admit it, many of us have been more like the rabbit, raccoon and Billy goat than the squirrel, but the past is behind us, and we must focus on the present. Are you ready to be what Gandhi referred to when he famously said, "Be the change you wish to see in the world?" Your outer reality is mirroring back your inner reality. If you are ready to make inner choices and take the inner risks to dream HUGE and put your whole heart, soul, energy, and talents into YOU, the game is won.

ask "am I ready?"

Am I ready to claim the glory?

Am I ready to take responsibility?

Am I ready to work as hard as necessary and put in the time?

Am I ready to give 100% of my self to the task?

Readiness is one of the key ingredients in realizing your potential and creating major opportunities in your life. Your willingness determines whether you will develop an attitude of gratitude for the actions you take in your life and all the possibilities that surround you. Be ready to love, forgive, laugh, dream, trust, give, be brave, stand alone if need be, and believe that all good things are possible, and already are!

I believe the greatest joy is in the journey. Destinations are always changing, so they never bring true satisfaction. We are always striving for more, and we are never satisfied. The key is to become the love and realize that the happiness is within. Then, the journey becomes the joy and the fun; then our work becomes play. When work is fun, everything is joyful. When we are doing something we love, or have an attitude of love, even digging a ditch can be fun, especially if we are doing it with someone we care about!

Being ready is all about embracing a dream and being prepared to welcome gifts from the universe. When the goal is clear, the energy appears!

Do you know what it means to be ready? It means having your ducks in a row, being prepared for whatever comes. It means being spiritually aware so that you can hear Spirit's messages. It means having the energy and health to meet any challenges that may come your way.

It doesn't work to do just enough to get by in the long run. I used to be the "just enough to get by" kid. For many years, I did just what was required, and just enough was all that I ever received. To be at the top of my game, I needed to think like an Olympic champion, be willing to give 100% to the goal of my passions.

The critical component to claiming your power is to be ready. You won't be able to reach your full potential if you are battling old demons. Now is the time to clear old blocks, to reframe old stories. Now is the time to research anything you may need to know to make your dreams reality. Preparation is key. It's like painting. The prep work is everything!

Now is the time to heal all of your past hurts so you can move forward without all that baggage. You must be willing to forgive yourself and others for anything in your past so that it will not hold you back. We hold on to these judgments we have made about ourselves and our egos like to remind us of them often. "Remember when you sounded like an idiot that time?" Then you become the idiot. But you can just let that judgment go by doing self-forgiveness. It may sound insincere at first, but the more you do it, the more it starts to sink in. You may have heard that it takes twenty-one days to form a new habit, and a health psychology researcher at University College London, Phillippa Lally, just found that it actually takes 66 days, so don't feel bad if it takes a while before your self-forgiveness seems to be working. Rest assured, if you forgive yourself for all the judgments of yourself and others about a million times, they will begin to sink in. You will start to ponder when you last had a critical self-thought.

☆ Tyler Perry

Tyler Perry, a writer, producer, and performer, is one of the most commercially successful African American filmmakers in history. Tyler Perry Studios, which opened in Atlanta in 2008, is the first major film studio in the nation to be owned by an African American. Tyler Perry is best known for his signature character, Madea. He is an example of a person who had a vision and prepared himself and followed it. He is famous for saying,

> ### "Anything you want is possible."
> *– Tyler Perry*

Born in New Orleans, Louisiana as "Emmitt Perry, Jr.," Tyler Perry was raised in poverty and suffered physical abuse at the hands of his father. He said his father's answer to everything was to "beat it out of you." In an effort to escape the violence, he attempted suicide as a teen. At sixteen, wanting to distance himself from his father, he changed his first name to Tyler. After dropping out of high school, he obtained his GED.

Tyler Perry had a fire inside of him. He realized early on that he must focus on one vision. In his mid-twenties, he saw an Oprah Winfrey Show that focused on the therapeutic power of writing, and he began journaling. His writing became his first play, *I Know I've Been Changed.* Tyler Perry went on to raise $12,000 by skimping and saving to finance the first production of his play at a community theatre when he was 22 years old. He said he was expecting a thousand people to show up for the show, but only thirty came.

However, he did not give up! Tyler Perry continued to work odd jobs while reworking the show. He staged the show in several other cities, but success still eluded him. Broke, he was living out of his car for a time. He continued to put on one show per year for several years until finally, his shows started to have a much bigger following. He says,

"There comes a time in your life when you've worked and you've stressed and you've tried to get there and you couldn't on your own but you have a dream and that dream has to take on the belief for you because you can't do it by yourself. Don't stop. Narrow your focus to one idea. One. And make it work. That will give birth to all the others. All you can do is plant the seed and water it. God himself has to give the increase. Only God can make the sunshine. Only God can bring the rain. But if you've planted the seed, you've done your part."

Tyler Perry has openly spoken about his belief that it is vital to keep focused on one thing and pour energy into it. He comments that people today spread their focus so thin on so many goals that they don't end up achieving any one of them. He attributes all of his success to the grace of God. By 2005, *Forbes* reported that he had sold "more than $100 million in tickets, $30 million in videos and an estimated $20 million in merchandise." He is one of the highest paid men in entertainment.

☆ Liz Murray

You may remember Liz Murray from the Lifetime movie, "Homeless to Harvard," which was based on her life. Born in the Bronx, New York to poor, drug-addicted parents, both of whom later contracted HIV, Liz said about growing up with her parents and sister, "We ate ice cubes because it felt like eating. We split a tube of toothpaste between us for dinner."

She said, "Everything was filthy and the drugs were everywhere. I used to go into the kitchen and see my parents shooting up cocaine; they didn't try to hide it. I would sit on the window sill, and stare out into the alley."

> ## "I was one of those people on the streets you walk away from."
> *– Liz Murray*

When Liz was fifteen, she became homeless, and a few years later, her mother died of Aids. She had an epiphany when she was looking at her mother's plain, donated coffin with her misspelled name scribbled on top in marker. When her friend fixed the spelling, she thought to herself, "It's now or never." Although she was living on the streets and riding the subways all night to stay warm, a fire had been lit inside her. She finished high school in two years, was awarded a New York Times scholarship for needy students, and was accepted into Harvard University from which she graduated!

In 2010, Liz published her autobiography, "Breaking Night" and went on to become a motivational speaker. She is the founder and director of "Manifest Living" and received an honorary doctorate of public service.

> "If I could have a family and a home one night, and all of it's gone the next, that must mean that life has the capacity to change. And then I thought, *'Whoa! That means that just as change happens to me, I can cause change in my life.'"*
> *− Liz Murray*

practice, routine, and commitment

Say these intentions aloud and write your own.

It is my intention to take care of myself.

It is my intention to study and train hard.

It is my intention to wake up early and stay up late until I finish what I started.

It is my intention to increase my knowledge.

It is my intention to look through the eyes of love.

It is my intention to see every moment positively.

It is my intention to use everything for learning.

It is my intention to meditate, focus, and live a healthy lifestyle.

1.

2.

3.

 make these quotes your own

Apply these quotes to your personal life.

Quote:

"Knowing is not enough; I must apply. Willing is not enough; I must do." -Johann Wolfgang von Goethe

Personalization Example:

"Knowing how to get good grades in my program at UCLA is not enough. I must work to reach my full potential."

Quotes to Personalize:

"Where the willingness is great, the difficulties cannot be great." -Niccolò Machiavelli

"Darkness cannot drive out darkness; only light can do that. Hate cannot drive out hate; only love can do that." -Martin Luther King, Jr.

"When a deep injury is done to us, we never heal until we forgive." - Alan Paton

"One secret of success in life is for a man to be ready for his opportunity when it comes." -Benjamin Disraeli

"Leadership is the readiness to stand out in a crowd."
- John C. Maxwell

"The enlightened give thanks for what most people take for
granted. . . granted, that vibration of gratitude makes you more
receptive to good in your life"- Michael Beckwith

an affirmation

I am pure divine energy, creating infinite possibilities and
opportunities with the intention to win naturally. I take full
responsibility for my choices and my unlimited potential,
the power of source energy within me right now. I express
joyfully and lovingly my gifts and talents with the world,
and I recognize that it is my role to give and the earth's
role to rejoice in my gifts. It is my role to share, and it is
the earth's role to receive. I accept from earth prosperity,
love, and faith, knowing that it reflects only what is in my
heart! So be it!

write your own affirmation

8

play your part

*"All the world's a stage and all the men and women
merely players" - William Shakespeare*

People may not remember Annie Sullivan while everyone remembers Helen Keller, but Annie Sullivan was the angel who taught Helen, who devoted her life to helping Helen realize her full potential. She is one of the unsung heroes. The fact is, we may all be unsung heroes.

Mother Teresa said,

"Not all of us can do great things. But we can do small things with great love."

Whether we end up being the leading players or supporting cast members, our contribution is important. Behind every great inventor, leader, doctor, entertainer, athlete, humanitarian, or anyone who has shared their gifts and talents with the world, there is someone who has helped or inspired them. The most valuable person is not always the person you have read about in the history books, newspapers, magazines, movies, or on social media. The most important person may be the one who inspired or mentored them. If I could ask all of these people, "Who helped you reach your goal?" they would give you at least one name. We all have gifts to share, and we are all standing on each other's shoulders. I am more valuable than I can imagine. You are more valuable than you can imagine. Our presence in this world is a gift.

Think of an entertainer, leader, or inventor who has greatly benefited the world. Imagine if that person never took responsibility for their gifts and choices. Without that person, the world would be a different place. What would the world be like without Beethoven, Shakespeare, Picasso, or George Washington Carver? What would the world be without the people who had the creativity and drive to invent the wheel, the car, or the airplane?

What would the world be without the person or people who helped these visionaries? What if they were never born? How would all of our lives be different?

positive projections

A positive projection is when we have a belief about ourselves and we assign it to someone else because it is too hard to look at in ourselves. Sometimes we judge the qualities of another person as "too good." We don't want to judge ourselves too positively, so we admire these qualities in others. If you strongly admire someone, you are resonating with the same quality you see in them that you have within yourself. If you didn't have it in yourself, you wouldn't even notice it in the other person, much less admire it.

I respect and look up to so many leaders: Mother Teresa, Gandhi, Martin Luther King, Cesar Chavez, Dalai Lama, Nelson Mandela, Barack Obama, Albert Einstein, Rosa Parks, Malcolm X, Opera Winfrey, Helen Keller, Harriet Tubman, Brian Stevenson, and countless others.

☆Bryan Stevenson

Founder and Executive Director of the Equal Justice Initiative in Montgomery, Alabama, Bryan Stevenson is a widely acclaimed public interest lawyer who has dedicated his life to helping the poor, the incarcerated and the condemned.

Bryan has successfully argued several cases in the United States Supreme Court and recently won a historic ruling that mandatory life-without-parole sentences for all children 17 or younger are unconstitutional. With his staff, he has won reversals, relief, or release for over 125 wrongly condemned prisoners on death row. He has spearheaded anti-poverty and anti-discrimination efforts and worked to educate communities about slavery, lynching and racial segregation. A Professor at the New York University School of Law, he has won dozens of prestigious awards; a list as long as your arm!

"You don't change the world with the ideas in your mind, but with the conviction in your heart."
– Bryan Stevenson

Mr. Stevenson has received 29 honorary doctoral degrees, including ones from Harvard, Yale, Princeton, and Oxford University. He is the author of the critically acclaimed New York Times bestseller, *Just Mercy*.

In his 2014 TED talk, Bryan discusses the scope of the problem of incarceration, and particularly that of men of color, in our country. He says,

> "In 1972, there were 300,000 people in jails in our country. Now there are 2.3 million! One out of three black men age 18-30 is in jail, prison, or on probation or parole. In urban communities, 50-60% of all young men of color are in jail or prison or on probation or parole."

Bryan decided to do everything he could to change these statistics!

When Bryan was a young lawyer, he had the honor of meeting Rosa Parks occasionally when she came to Montgomery to meet with her friends, Johnnie Carr, the organizer of the Montgomery Bus Boycott and Virginia Durr whose husband represented Martin Luther King. Rosa asked Bryan to describe what he was doing, and he explained that he was trying to get people off of death row and get teenagers released from prison who had been tried as adults.

Rosa Parks said to him, "That's gonna make you tired, tired, tired," to which Johnnie Carr added,

> "That's why you've got to be Brave, Brave, Brave!"

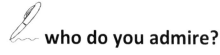

who do you admire?

They are a positive projection of YOU. You wouldn't admire them if you didn't possess the same qualities.

Write out the name of someone you admire:

What do you admire most about them?

How are you like them?

How can you use their example to tap into your own unlimited potential?

allow the universe to unfold your future

If you can imagine and prepare yourself, the whole universe will turn every moment into an opportunity for your transformation. You don't need to know every detail (or any detail) of how the opportunities are going to be made available. All you need to do is joyfully visualize great possibilities and simply allow them to unfold. According to *The Law of Attraction*, you have an attractor field that is already bringing everything to you.

The truth is there is no one greater or lesser and vice versa than you. There's no one and nothing that you have to defeat so that you can feel better about yourself, except your own fear and insecurity that you project on the world. Have you noticed that you compare yourself to others to discover who you are? Do you use other people as a frame of reference to judge yourself? For example, I only interpreted myself as poor because I compared myself to those I interpreted as rich.

The key phrase to know when you are comparing yourself is, "I think I am this because I think you/they are that." You are allowing your interpretations about the world and the people in it to affect you. In each moment, you have an opportunity to be aware of the *Law or Reflection* by looking inside first at the source of all beliefs. If you change the way you look at things, the things you look at will change.

> "Life's most persistent and
> urgent question is:
> What are you doing for others?"
> - *Martin Luther King, Jr.*

you are powerful!

As you enjoy the process of visualizing yourself achieving and having your goals, use your imagination to visualize yourself fine-tuning your skills as if the end goal was happening now. Feel it, see it, hear it, smell it, taste it, and know it is happening. Feel your success down to the smallest detail in your heart. As you take action from a place of confidence, you will then begin to experience the physical equivalent of your positive emotions.

learn from everything

Appreciate and take full advantage of all the opportunities in your life provided by teachers, mentors, guides, trainers, and even opponents. Stay open to life's lessons as they come, remembering that life never is all for your benefit and use everything to expand your consciousness. Life is providing opportunities for you to grow and develop into your authentic *full potential self.* When you fully commit to learning from whatever opportunity comes across your path, you'll continually find yourself in the right place at the right time because you are prepared.

To embrace the power of opportunity is to know that it's not some fickle or mysterious force that's going to knock on your door someday in the future. Opportunities are always reflections, and it is up to you to be aware of them in each moment. People who succeed at their goals don't wait for the opportunity to show up first before they start preparations. They "fake it until they make it." They prepare as if the goal or prize has already manifested. The old saying goes, "When opportunity meets preparation, success is certain."

You may not always recognize an opportunity, for it can disguise itself as failure, mistakes, accidents, hardships, abuse, imprisonment, and abandonment. I wasn't aware that failing the first and second grade was an opportunity for me to focus more because I couldn't just surf through school with little effort. I had to hone my attention in order to do what came easily for other kids. I didn't realize that the difficulties in my childhood were gifts that would prove to me my incredible strength and capability. I didn't realize that it was an opportunity for me to accept myself unconditionally.

I still experience occasional fears and doubts, but now I know they are just passing thoughts and I can overcome them. I can stop what I'm doing and make peace with them. I can love myself right where I stand and see the love inside of myself reflected in every moment.

When you begin to follow the love, excitement, and guidance within your heart, opportunities will manifest effortlessly. Loving thoughts will translate into your actions and will create the awareness of what I call a "natural winner," someone who's winning comes from an authentic and limitless source. Seeing every moment as an opportunity creates a *natural winner* mentality. Are you still waiting for the perfect moment? The perfect moment is now.

I am that I am

If I am choosing my thoughts, then I am choosing my truth as expressed in the well-known Hebrew phrase translated as "I am that I am." (This is also translated as "I am what I am" and "I create what I create"). If I choose to believe that I am limited, my life will reflect my truth and be limited. If I choose to think that I am an unlimited and boundless powerful being, then my life will reflect that truth instead.

You can choose to believe that you are responsible for what is possible in your life. As you accept that you are responsible for the opportunities that come your way, you can choose to take responsibility for your willingness to create the life you want to live. When you decide to take responsibility for your ability to focus thought energy on your heart desires, you will know you are co-creating with the divine source.

quotes to reflect on:

"We are addicted to our thoughts. We cannot change anything if we cannot change our thinking." - Santosh Kalwar

"Any idea, plan, or purpose may be placed in the mind through repetition of thought." - Napoleon Hill

"What we do comes out of who we believe we are."- Rob Bell

"The mind is everything. What you think you become." - Buddha

"The ancestor of every action is a thought."- Ralph Waldo Emerson

are there quotes that have been meaningful to you?

9

it is possible

"Knock, And He'll open the door
Vanish, And He'll make you shine like the sun
Fall, And He'll raise you to the heavens
Become nothing, And He'll turn you into everything."
— Jalal Ad-Din Rumi

Are you willing to see yourself as a winner and fully step into your power, to harness the energy of God that is you? Are you willing to be the extraordinary person that you came onto this earth to be, to use your God-given talents and life experiences? Are you ready to be of full service to the world by allowing yourself to use what you have been given to your fullest capacity? Are you willing to put in the work?

Consider how these superstars exceeded what they ever dreamed possible.

☆ Tommy Caldwell

Tommy Caldwell was developmentally delayed when he was a baby and didn't even start to crawl until after he was two years old. He was told he might be mentally retarded, but his father didn't give up on him. He thought it would make sense to "toughen" Tommy up, so he took him skiing and rock climbing. By the time Tommy was sixteen years old, he had won "Snowbird," the International Sport Climbing Championship, shocking the rock climbing world. He climbed a wall that no other climber, professional or other, was able to scale!

A year or two later, as a teenager, he was invited to Kyrgyzstan with a group of young climbers and taken hostage at gunpoint for six days before pushing one of his captors off a cliff (the man lived, but it allowed Tommy's group to escape). Then, in his twenties, he chopped off his finger in a carpentry accident and was told by those who knew about climbing that he would never be able to climb again; the finger was too critical for the hand-holds. However, he didn't let it stop him. He had been trying to climb a particularly challenging route before the accident and could not do it. But, after the accident, he drew on his inner strength, amped up his training, and he was able to complete the climb!

Tommy and his climbing partner went on to be the first (and only) climbers to conquer the Dawn Wall, the most challenging (and formerly deemed impossible to climb) face of Half Dome. And Tommy did it without a finger!

About his experience being held captive, Tommy said,

"Ever since Kyrgyzstan, I just had this fire in me that is different from anything I've had before...I felt something come over me, this reserve of energy, this confidence like I knew I was cold, I knew I was hungry, but those things didn't matter anymore. I realized that my preconceived limits were totally off base, that we are capable of so much more than we could ever imagine."

Tommy harnessed all his energy to put into working the problem and achieving his goal. His experience is captured in the documentary *The Dawn Wall*. What is not told in the film is that, before the historic climb, he had reached his lowest point and was about to scale the mountain without any ropes at all, a suicide mission. What stopped him? He took his despair and anguish and transmuted the energy into source to achieve a miraculous climb.

☆ Amy Purdy

Snowboarding became a passion for Amy Purdy when she was fifteen. However, when she was nineteen, she contracted bacterial meningitis and had to have both of her legs amputated below the knees. The doctors only gave her a two percent chance of survival due to her advanced sepsis. However, survive she did, and two years later, she received a kidney transplant from her father, who also co-founded a non-profit organization called Adaptive Action Sports. Amy has been an inspiration to many. She is a two-time

Paralympian and received silver and bronze medals in the 2018 and 2014 Games. She exemplifies enthusiasm! She participated on "Dancing With the Stars" and was a contestant on "The Amazing Race" with her husband as her partner.

☆ Wim Hoff

Known as the "Iceman," Wim Hoff won 21 Guinness World Records, ran a half marathon about the Arctic Circle with no shoes and wearing only shorts, and climbed the highest mountains in the world similarly clad! He swam 66 meters under ice and ran a marathon through the Namib Desert without drinking. He is living proof that one can accomplish anything if they put their mind to it and put energy into training.

> ### "What I am capable of, everybody can learn."
> ### - *Wim Hoff*

It's our natural inclination to say, "That's impossible!" We want to believe that it can't be done, but it's all in our minds! There are so many examples of people who have done unthinkably extraordinary things.

Tommy Caldwell, Amy Purdy, and Wim Hoff were natural winners. Tommy's dad was his mentor, the one whose shoulders he stood on. He took Tommy hiking when he was young to strengthen him and was his climbing partner when, as an adult, he was recovering from his divorce and a severed finger. Amy Purdy's "mentor" was her father, who helped with her recovery and started a foundation in her name.

see yourself as a child

Sometimes others believe in us and can see our light and potential for extraordinary achievement when we cannot see it. Others can see the love that we are when we cannot.

When my grandmother died, I came into possession of boxes of photos and paperwork, but I didn't go through them. Recently, I picked them up and found a picture of myself taken when I was about nine months old. I was just sitting up. How cute I was! I was struck by how innocent I looked and, suddenly, I was flooded with overwhelming love and compassion for myself.

At that moment, I thought to myself, "I would never harm this little kid," and yet I was harming myself. I thought, "I would never speak unkindly to this child," and yet I was speaking very critically to myself. I would never have thought of killing this child, and yet I had come close to taking my own life. I would never have abandoned this child, but I had abandoned myself. At that moment, I realized that I was the answer to my own prayers. All I needed was to see myself as this child. He still exists inside of me. And your child still exists inside of you.

I put the picture in a prominent place in my apartment and decided to send him love daily. I had a dialogue with my child. I had conversations back and forth, telling him that I loved him. By doing this, I was able to heal my younger self and clear up any misunderstandings he may have formed. I told him, "Mom loved you. Grandma loved you. I love you. I will never leave you or abandon you. I would even give my life for you. I have given my life for you—by living! "

When we send love back in time to the moment where misunderstandings began, we heal the root from which all of the trauma and drama began. When the roots are healthy, everything that springs from them becomes healthy. In this way, I was able to recast the way I felt about myself. I was able to change my perception of myself in a way that made it possible for me to truly love myself.

look with the eyes of love

The easiest way to solve a problem is to eliminate it. My "problem" was that I saw myself in a distorted way. Once I saw myself as a beautiful, innocent child, I could no longer feel judgment about myself and all of the self-criticism and stories of lack instantly disappeared. It was like the veil of separation was instantly lifted, the curtain that was blocking the true action of my life was removed, and I could see clearly for the first time. I could see myself as THE love, possessing the positive qualities that other people had attributed to me.

I told my younger self that, no matter what challenges come his way, he is strong enough to meet them. He is bigger than any problem. He has been equipped with the armor of God to withstand any challenge and any setback. He was born to let his light shine, to win. He was born to shine, to succeed, and to serve. He is made of God so he can only be beautiful, and things do not establish his worth. He is worthy because he was born. He already has approval; he doesn't need to seek it externally. He is intrinsically valuable.

can YOU see yourself through new eyes?

How have you been looking at yourself? Do you have a photo of yourself when you were a baby? Pull out some pictures of your younger self and put one on your fridge or somewhere you frequent, where you can look at it daily and send it love. Who couldn't love that smile? Look into those lovely eyes. What do you want to tell that child? Sit with the photo for several minutes and be present together.

Tell yourself how much you love your little self. You can also write a supportive letter to him or her. Tell your child that you will always be there with him or her because you live inside of each other. Your child may have felt alone and scared when young, but he or she is with you now. You are an adult and can take care of him or her.

 complete these statements

If I saw myself with all the love with which I see my little child, I would be able to...

If I truly felt safe, I would…

If I knew that I was LOVE, I would…

If I truly believed in myself, I would be able to…

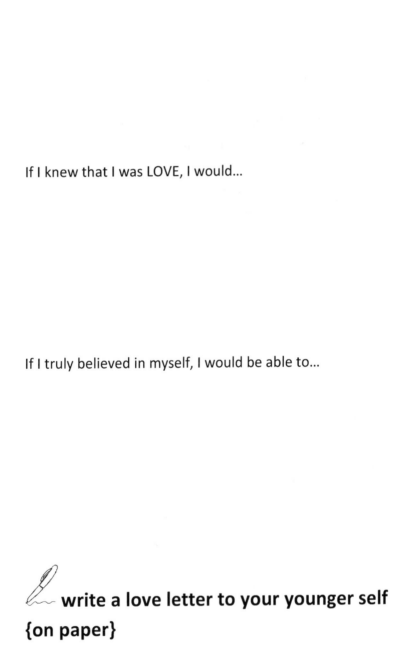 **write a love letter to your younger self {on paper}**

how are you going to use your winning energies?

Now that you see yourself clearly, how are you going to use your winning energies? If Tommy Caldwell, Amy Purdy, and Wim Hoff prove anything, it's that we have unlimited potential! Plus, in Tommy Caldwell and Amy Purdy's cases, their parents advocated for them and saw their incredible potential. Tommy Caldwell's father saw that he was struggling as a child and pushed him. He didn't accept that his child may not be able to achieve even though Tommy had been labeled as "slow." He pushed Tommy and eventually, Tommy learned to push himself. When Tommy lost his finger, he didn't accept what people were telling him; he continued to reach for his goals and achieved them!

What are you going to do with your incredible potential? Whether you are using your natural winning energies to achieve greatness or to help others achieve greatness, practice choices from a *natural winner* mindset. Your focused, conscious energy will be the cause, and everything else will be the effect. If your mind wanders off uncontrollably, and sometimes you find yourself feeling sad or depressed for no apparent reason, it may be because your unfocused mind tends to pick up whatever thought forms are in alignment with your core emotional belief.

If you believe at the core of your being that you are not valuable or smart, then your mind will go back to the default button to which it is accustomed. That is why it important to develop a positive routine every day even though you may feel a lot of resistance. Your old habits and labels are going to try to stop you by coming up with excuses to keep you from changing the life you are used to living. Negative or challenging situations will show up demanding your attention, but they are just trying to derail you from the task at hand. These ego games are intended to keep you feeling and playing small.

The secret is that all the energy in the universe is at your disposal, and everything already exists in energy form. The earth you live on is energy, the galaxy you live in is energy, the universe is energy, and you're energy. Therefore, you have unlimited access to unlimited energy if you're willing to accept it and focus your mind on possibilities. Energy cannot be created or destroyed; it can only be transformed. Use the power of your mind to consciously and consistently focus on the feeling of the end game happening now, what you truly desire to manifest. Visualize and feel the goal, and the journey will take care of itself. All energies are neutral; it's what you choose to use those energies for that gives the energy meaning. If the energy you're experiencing feels depressing, it is an indicator that you're using your energy for negative thinking. Instead, you can choose now to reach for a contrasting energy thought that feels empowering and joyful.

Negative feelings make you aware that you need to choose a loving energy thought that you want to see manifested in your life. The body, mind, and emotions are tools to experience the different interpretations of energies. You know what you want by knowing what you don't want. That is how you create the world around you with unconscious and conscious energy. The world you experience is only a reflection of your thoughts.

You can become anything you want to be in the present moment if you are willing to focus your thought energy. When you label yourself as being only human, your life will reflect human limitations. When you label yourself as being an infinite spiritual being, your life will reflect that awareness of an infinite spiritual being in physical form. You are pure divine energy, and you can focus your energy in any direction you want. You're not your body or mind, but pure divine thought energy. Would you make different choices if you believed that you are a powerful spiritual being? Would you dream bigger and reach for higher goals? Yes! All your actions stem from your thoughts and thoughts make up your self-concept.

In the past, you may have believed that you were the manifestation of the ego and not pure divine energy. Whenever we label ourselves, we're placing a spell of limitation on who we are and what we can become. Limited thoughts can only create a limited self. Some people may have placed limited labeling upon us, but the label or spell can only work if we give our energy to it by believing it is true.

Ask yourself, "Is this label benefiting or harming me in any way?" Don't spend energy trying to remove or fight labels because it only gives them power. The more you focus energy on anything, the more power you give to it. Instead of saying, "I am not weak," say, "I am not that weak, and I am getting stronger every moment." As you begin practicing a positive routine and start looking for places in your life where you have the power of choice, you will develop a natural winner's mindset and start feeling, walking, standing, acting, and even smiling like a natural winner.

Ask yourself, "What would a powerful, intelligent, natural winner do in a situation like this?"

limit the limiting self-talk

Negative self-talk limits us! It is the reason for much of our struggle. We don't attempt to do new things because of the limitation we place on ourselves. When we focus on fears and doubts instead of the knowledge that we're powerful beyond measure, we feel stuck. Tommy Caldwell had this very epiphany when he met and surmounted challenges in Kyrgyzstan beyond what he had ever experienced in the past. He realized he had so much more potential than he ever dreamed possible.

If you don't know what you're capable of being, doing, or having, you stop dreaming of being more than what you already are. However, you can just let that story of limitation go. You don't need to go to Kyrgyzstan. You don't need to cut off a finger. You don't need to be traumatized or abused. You just need to wake up to the reality of your limitless ability and believe completely and unwaveringly in yourself.

Choose to believe "I can" and "I am" instead of "I can't" and "I'm not." Choose to believe in possibilities instead or impossibilities. Choose to believe in your unlimited potential instead of a limited self. Whatever you believe and feel, you will be.

You have to be willing to be called an "insane fool" by the naysayers projecting limitations on you. As you choose to reverse your thinking process from "when I see it... I'll believe it," to "when I believe in my focused thought to create my life from within…. I will create it," you will begin to take a seemingly impossible goal and realize it is within your grasp. Choose to live your life as if your success is guaranteed.

real success

Real success is on the inside; it has nothing to do with objects or anything outside of us. There are a lot of wealthy people who aren't happy. People may have incredible material success but have little success on the inside or in their relationships and personal lives. Isn't true success based on the amount of love that you can let in and experience? Isn't true abundance expressed in one's radiant smile?

You get to choose to live your life as if you're already the joyful recipient of that success, that love. You can be more, do more, and live more when you have love, enthusiasm, and joy at the foundation of all your actions. You get to practice doing an activity with the intention of love flowing into every movement. You get to practice loving and appreciating every breath and how it sustains your life without you ever thinking about it. Take a moment and practice feeling your breath. As you breathe in and out, think, "I am thankful for this breath."

Whatever you do with love as it's foundation will increase your awareness of love energy, focus, and that power. It will strengthen your knowledge of the unlimited potential within. It will inspire and transform your experience as a conscious creator of your reality. You get to choose to keep doing what you're doing but can do it with an attitude of gratitude, appreciation, and love.

A natural winner mindset has as it's foundation a natural

and constant feeling of love and appreciation for this ever-present creative energy force. When you're walking, talking, reading, working, driving, bathing, baking a cake, or putting on your shoes, become aware of this unlimited force. Practice this every day until it comes as natural as breathing.

what does "real success" mean to you?

clean your lens of perception

Perception is the ability to see, hear, or become aware of something through the senses. It is as if you went to the cinema to watch a movie and believed that what you were experiencing was originating from the screen in front of you and not the projector behind you.

The cinema represents the world, the screen represents your interpretation, and the projector represents your thoughts. The images on the screen represent your perception. You're sharing the earth with other people, and yet the life you're experiencing is different. It is like everyone is at an amusement park on the same ride, but we are all experiencing it differently. Some of us are having fun, others are depressed or stressed, and others are celebrating and taking responsibility for the way they feel.

I see the world with the interpretation of my eyes, I touch the world with the interpretation of my hands, and I perceive the world with the interpretation of my mind. I give meaning to the world I see, feel, touch, hear, taste, and smell, and yet it is all filtered through the beliefs I hold within my mind. It's done unto us as we perceive it to be. We laugh and cry only because we believe what we see on the screen is real. The truth is the entire time the movie is happening inside of the projector on the wall behind us.

As you begin to realize that your life is like that of a movie projector projecting your thoughts into the universe and creating your world, you will no longer look outside of yourself for the approval of others. You will stop giving your power and energy away, and you will no longer allow yourself to be labeled as a victim since you know that you have authored and directed your own life so no one else can be held responsible. What happens within the mind is more important than what happens to the body because the body and worldly items don't define who you are; the mind does. You create who you are and what you want to be in this life with your mind, then you project it on the screen of your life, like the movie.

the gifts already are

There was a time when I was living in a dark night of depression. My car had been repossessed, and I was about to get evicted from my apartment. The harder I tried to find work, the more rejections I got until I couldn't get out of bed. I lay in a dark room, praying and crying, feeling helpless and alone for a month. I felt like I was experiencing the death of my dreams with no hope in sight. I was about to give up because I had no money and, the more I thought about my dark situation, the deeper I went into depression. My mind took me to fearful places where I wanted to end it all.

At that moment, my depression turned to anger, and I was ready to accept my fate. If I was to lose everything that I had worked for, then so be it! If I was going to be evicted from my Hollywood apartment with no money, food, or love, so be it! But something about being willing to give it all up gave me strength. I was no longer afraid of losing everything, being homeless, or dying alone, and peace came over me, I was in acceptance. I stopped fighting the fear and depression. I was willing to give it all up and allow life to hit me with its best shot and, suddenly, I had new strength!

I no longer wanted to escape from what I thought was my miserable and painful life. I was willing to take the hit and get back up and get hit again and again. I wasn't going to run from the fear of the worst thing that could happen to me. I realized that my depression and fear were a reflection of me being scared to lose everything. I had grown up in that situation and knew it well. I realized that I was more afraid of going back to the poverty of my childhood than anything else. I was worried that the future was going to be like the pain of the past. As strange as it seems, my anger transformed into bravery and I lay in bed still, but unafraid. I felt relaxed and a feeling of surrender. I was no longer giving into self-hatred and defeatist thoughts. Having the willingness to lose everything gave me the courage to face disparity. There is nothing wrong with failure, but it is the fear of it that destroys the possibility of success. The feelings of lack and fear go out into the universal attractor field and draw it in.

Right then, at five o'clock on a Friday evening, I got a phone call from my agent who said, "You have an $80,000 check waiting for you. Your Pepsi commercial went worldwide!" My check would be available to pick up a few days later! My depression instantly disappeared, and I began to laugh and cry at the same time. My state of mind changed, and I became happy and hopeful.

The reason I tell this story is that the only thing that changed in my life was that I suddenly had hope. There wasn't any money in my account yet, but suddenly everything felt different. How is it that depression can instantly lift? Positive thoughts bring positive energy. Negative thoughts drain precious life energy.

My depression came from the thought energy that I was broke and didn't have enough to survive. Joy came from a thought that money was available in my agent's office. It easy to believe that outside circumstances and situations dictate one's emotional state, but the truth is thoughts dictate emotions. I was buying into lack mentality, thinking that there wasn't enough for me, an old story I had been telling myself. Even before I found out about the check, I could have bought into trust and abundance instead. I could have assumed that the universe would always take care of me, which is the truth.

The real power is in the energy used to focus on a goal and being in the present moment. Instead of laying in bed for a month being depressed, I could have been hopeful and joyfully pursued my goal. I took myself through unnecessary mental pain because I chose to create a dark story about a gloomy future life instead of a tale about accomplishment with an end resulting in me standing in victory. I had little faith in myself. I abandoned all the years of studying spiritual and self-help books. It all came down to focusing on the only moment anyone can live, and that is NOW. There is powerful energy at work in life that is greater than the darkest fears. Live it now! This is your time of power!

How much do you know about your life? Do you know where your choices are going to lead? Do you know what is best for you from a human point of view? How many times have you picked someone to be in your life for one reason, and it didn't turn out the way you wanted? How can you know that a choice you are making is right for you when you don't know the end of your story? Could it be that, from a spiritual viewpoint, every choice you make is expanding and benefitting you, carrying you towards a specific ultimate destination? Could it be that you don't know what's good or bad for you because it is all relative? We define *good* and *bad*. From our human perspective, something might seem to be "bad" or not assisting us in going in the direction of our dreams, but do we know the universe's plan for us? Could we just consider that everything is for our highest good?

Having confidence that everything is as it should be and you are on track is necessary to win naturally. You must believe a plan is in action and the results already are, you just haven't realized them yet. They are already manifested in God's eyes, even if you may not see them in your reality yet.

practice winning naturally

The power to focus your thoughts is the power to focus your life energy. To master things around you, you must master the thoughts within you about those things. Focus your mind, emotion, and actions on a skill until it becomes effortless. Use your focused thoughts and energy to manifest the awareness of more happiness and prosperity within your life.

Have faith, knowing that the gifts already are. They are already manifested in the mind and heart even before they materialize in physical reality. According to the *Law of Creation*, within you is the creative source of everything that will be experienced in your world. It is done unto you as you believe. It is you that defines yourself, and it is you that gives your life meaning. Change your thoughts and emotions on the inside to love, and your life will reflect it on the outside. No exceptions.

 read and reflect on these quotes

"Energy and persistence conquer all things." - Ben Franklin

"There's enough for everyone. If you believe it, if you can see it, if you act from it, it will show up for you. That's the truth."
- Michael Bernard Beckwith

"Miracles start to happen when you give as much energy to your dreams as you do to your fears." - Richard Wilkins

"The energy we put out is the energy we get back." -Rachael Bermingham

"The secret of change is to focus all of your energy, not on fighting the old, but on building the new."-Dan Millman

what the heck do you want? No holds barred! Go for it! {on paper}

Go inside your heart and ask, "What is my purpose?" What am I here for? What do I want to achieve? What is my wildest dream? If money was no object and you could do ABSOLUTELY anything, what would it be?

It's time to

...be outrageous

...be unreasonable

...dream HUGE

...harness all of your emotions and

...turn them into drive and productivity

You can do it!

10

this is YOUR chapter

"Whatever you can do, or dream you can do, begin it. Boldness has genius, power, and magic in it. Begin it now." - Goethe

The universe is yours—it was made for your pleasure. You were born to be a light, to be the sun. You were born to be the champion of your own dreams. SO WAKE UP. It's time to shine. It's time to cast off the cloak of insecurity and fear and claim your destiny. You are more powerful than you can possibly imagine. SO WAKE UP. You are creating all the time, but you get to decide what you are manifesting through your intention, your willingness, and your gratitude. You are the architect, the painter, the cinematographer, the poet, and the director. Be your own muse!

Now that you are *woke,* you get to choose how you respond to what life brings to you. You get to give it meaning since all the meaning that anything has is what you have given it. You are the master! This is more than just your chapter, this is your life, your moment to make your dreams happen. What will you do with your pencil, your paintbrush, your beautiful heart and soul? What will you gift to the world? What will you gift to yourself, knowing that you are one with the universe and everything you give comes back multiplied? So give all you can and be thankful for the gifts that come back to you. You are like a flame that can light a million candles and lose nothing because we all have infinite resources. You can dip into the universal pool of energy and claim its fire for yourself. You can direct it towards your heartfelt ideas and projects, and it will fuel them.

It's time to make a plan! It's time to infuse your dreams with tons of energy, vision, commitment, and intention. It's time to take a step...just one step in the direction of your dreams!

As Chinese philosopher, Lao Tzu said, "A journey of a thousand miles begins with a single step."

What step can you take right now?

Hello? Are you still there?

Not sure what to do? Here are some suggestions for exercises you can do right now.

- Heart-gazing
- Positive self-talk
- Affirmations
- Gratitude/Appreciation
- Automatic writing and journaling
- Write a letter to your younger self
- Have your future self write your current self a letter
- Make a list of your goals
- Describe your wildest dreams
- Complete the sentence, "If I could have anything…"
- Refer to all the exercises in this book
- Redefine experiences that you may have viewed as negative in a more positive light
- Move your body/exercise
- Meditate
- Focus on your breath
- Ask yourself, "What would love do?"
- Set an intention for how you want to feel and what you want to achieve
- Remember, love is an inside job and you have to fill yourself up so you can give from your overflow. You are the love. You are the gift. So be it.